The Second Marriage Guidebook

Dealing with the Unique
Factors of the Second Wedding

GEORGE W. KNIGHT

JM Publications
A Division Of
JM PRODUCTIONS
P.O. BOX 837 • BRENTWOOD, TN 37027

Contents

INTRODUCTION

Gone are the days when remarriages were hurriedly planned and the couple repeated their vows before a justice of the peace in a simple ceremony. Today, they want a more elaborate ceremony that gives their wedding a lively spirit of celebration. This trend has developed in recent years with the dramatic increase in the number of second-time weddings. Nationally, three of every ten marriages today is a remarriage for one or both parties.

In spite of the boom in second-time weddings, too many couples marry again without thinking through the practical side of their remarriage relationship. This brings us around to the purpose of this book—to help you think about some of the realities of marriage "the second time around." This includes everything from planning an appropriate wedding ceremony, to merging two households into one, to learning to get along with stepchildren. Remarriage is different than a first-time trip to the matrimonial altar. This book underscores those differences and alerts you to the need to get prepared.

My thanks to the remarried couples who talked frankly with me about their experiences to give this book its practical, realistic flavor. They have shown that one of the secrets of a successful remarriage is an attitude of total honesty with each other, tempered with the spirit of love.

George W. Knight

1
Thinking Straight About Remarriage

All her "formerly married" friends call her Julie. They used to have such great times together. But recently Julie has been turning down their social invitations to spend more and more time with Hank. She and Hank have even hinted at the possibility of getting married later in the year.

Five years ago Julie would have scoffed at the idea that another "special man" could ever become a part of her life. Her first experience with marriage and, as it turned out, an insecure and demanding husband, left her bitter and disillusioned. Hank seems to be cut from a different piece of cloth, but she wonders if she can really be sure. Is she ready at last to give marriage another try? Or, should she hold off a while longer to make sure this relationship is right for her?

If you have been through a divorce, you can probably identify with Julie's mixed feelings. A broken marriage is such a traumatic experience for most people that they vow never to put themselves in a position where they can be hurt that badly again. These emotional scars eventually heal, but the process takes time. This is why it's better to be overcautious about saying "I do" the second time than to rush headlong into a new relationship.

At the same time, don't let your caution become such an obsession that it cancels out your chances for happiness and success in a second marriage. Thousands of couples before you have built enriching and rewarding marriages the second time around. One unfortunate marital experience doesn't condemn you to perpetual failure in love and marriage. Use the lessons you have learned from your previous marriage to build the foundation for a lasting and rewarding relationship.

So the first principle to keep in mind as you think about remarriage is this: *Don't be in a hurry to say "I do," but work hard to stay positive and optimistic about the possibilities of a good second marriage.* This is only one of a number of important principles that should guide your thinking along the path toward remarriage. Check yourself against the following guidelines to make sure you are thinking straight about this important step in your life.

Analyze the Nature of Your Second-Marriage Relationship

Did you ever stop to think that remarriage comes in several different forms? The three basic types are: (1) two divorced people marrying each other; (2) a never-married person marrying a divorced person; and (3) a widowed person marrying a divorced or never-married person.

Each of these patterns features its own unique needs and demands. You and your fiancé should be aware of the category into which your relationship falls. This will help you anticipate some of the adjustments you might face after you are married.

1. *Two divorced people marrying each other.* At least 50 percent of all remarriages involve both a man and a woman who have been divorced from their previous mates. Remarriages of this type generally get off on an equal footing because both husband and wife have been through the personal anguish of a broken marriage. Both should be older, wiser, and more mature because of this experience. And both may have vowed that they will work harder at building a better relationship the second time around. All these are pluses that can serve them well and strengthen their chances of success in a second marriage.

But let's look at this type of remarriage from another perspective. Two divorced people are more likely to have children from each of their previous unions. If each has custody of their children, this could cause overcrowding of their household, as well as an extra

8

financial burden. Even if they don't have all their children together under the same roof, the husband may be making child-support payments to his ex-wife. This could become a real bone of contention in the remarriage relationship.

Some couples in this type of remarriage have even discovered that their determination to build a good relationship the second time around can actually hinder their success. One couple whom we'll call Irene and Harold are a good example of how this can happen. They are so afraid of the possibility of another broken marriage that they never discuss their differences. Every time a problem comes up, they suppress their true feelings and refuse to confront the issue.

This pattern of behavior could cause a backlog of resentment that will eventually overflow and swamp their marriage—the very thing they are trying to avoid. Irene and Harold need to learn that good marriages are built not by avoiding conflict but by dealing with their tensions in a healthy, realistic way. Conflict itself doesn't break up a marriage. In their case, the real enemy of a happy, fulfilling marriage is their unhealthy pattern of conflict resolution.

So if you are divorced and are marrying a person who has also been through a broken marriage, be aware of the things you have going for you as well as some of the subtle problems that could trip you up. This awareness can help your remarriage get off on the right foot.

2. *A never-married person marrying a divorced person.* The second type of remarriage occurs when a person who has never been married before unites with a person who has been through a divorce. Many couples in these situations are under the delusion that "love conquers all"—that the previous marital status of the husband and wife have little bearing on their chances for happiness and success.

A more realistic approach is to go into a marriage like this with your eyes wide open about some of the potential trouble spots. Armed with the facts, both of you will be better equipped to deal with the problems as they occur.

If you are the never-married party who is marrying a person who has been divorced, don't be surprised if your parents raise a howl of protest when you announce your intentions. Most parents want nothing but the best for their children. It may be hard for them to see how a divorced person could possibly be "the best" for their very deserving son or daughter.

Above all, try to keep your cool if your parents should react like this. In time, they may mellow in their opinion. If your parents' approval is very important to you, you might even consider a long engagement. This could give them the time they need to get to know your fiancé better and to accept your marriage with their blessing.

Children can also pose a special adjustment for remarried couples in this category. Becky and Marty have discovered this startling truth in their relationship. Marty was a bachelor until he met and married Becky, a divorced woman with two small children. They thought they had a thorough understanding about how they would relate to the children until Marty noticed how often Becky "gave in" to their demands.

Since Marty had never been a parent, he had little idea of what was appropriate behavior for children of this age. He accused Becky of "spoiling them rotten" with her permissive approach to discipline. She retaliated by reminding him that they were her children and she would treat them as she pleased.

Marty and Becky's conflict over the children finally grew so severe that they sought the help of a professional counselor. He led them to see that Marty was unrealistic in his expectation of the children, while Becky was too lenient. Her casual approach to discipline, he pointed out, probably stemmed from her guilt feelings about the trauma the children had experienced because of her divorce from their father.

After these truths surfaced, Marty and Becky were able to talk openly about the problem. They eventually settled on an approach to child-rearing that worked to the benefit of everyone in the family.

Parental coolness toward the marriage and different levels of expectation of the children are not unique, of course, to remarriages where one spouse has been divorced and the other has never been married. But these two particular problems do seem to be more pronounced in remarriages of this type. It's always better to be prepared for these adjustments than to be overwhelmed by shock or surprise when they happen.

3. *A widowed person marrying a divorced or never-married person.* Another pattern of remarriage involves a person who has lost his previous mate through death. Remarriages of this type seem to require little adjustment when two people who have been widowed marry each other. They approach each other on equal ground, so to speak, having emerged from a common experience. Each partner is more willing to let the other remember his or her good experiences from the previous marriage without feeling jealous or insecure. But a different dynamic enters the picture when a widowed person marries a divorced person or someone who has never been married before.

Let's illustrate by thinking of a typical couple, Helen and Wayne, who fit this category. Helen had been married to her first husband for about ten years when he was killed in a automobile accident. Since they had enjoyed a happy, successful relationship, Helen didn't even think about dating another man for the first four years after his death. Then she met Wayne and dated him steadily for a year or so before they were married. Wayne talked openly about his divorce, as though he and his ex-wife had parted amicably and were still good friends.

Within a few weeks after their marriage, both Wayne and Helen realized their relationship would require a lot of negotiation and adjustment. Helen idolized her former mate and even compared Wayne's behavior unfavorably to his when they got in a heated argument. Wayne resented her frequent references to her departed spouse and let her know in no uncertain terms that he would not be compared to a "dead man." As it turned out, Wayne's relationship with his ex-wife had been miserable and unfulfilling. He just couldn't understand how Helen could speak so positively of a mate from her past.

What Wayne and Helen are dealing with is a "ghost" from the past. And ghosts are always harder to reckon with than real people. In remarriages like theirs where a previous mate is deceased, the surviving partner almost always minimizes the faults of the departed and magnifies his or her good points. It's a part of the old superstition that you should never speak evil of those who have died.

Wayne may have little choice in this marriage but to let Helen hang on to her good memories of this "ghost" from the past without getting uptight and defensive. On the other hand, Helen needs to try to understand his feelings as her present marriage partner. No man likes to be compared unfavorably to another man—particularly a dead man whom he didn't even know. Many adjustments and compromises like these will have to be worked out patiently as their relationship matures.

The "ghost from the past" problem may be even worse in marriages where a widowed person unites with someone who has never been married before. The previously single partner has no practical marriage experience by which to judge his or her mate's memory of a past relationship. In the case of Wayne and Helen, at least Wayne had enough marital experience to realize that no marriage is perfect. He automatically knew that Helen wasn't telling the whole truth about her relationship with her former husband.

But this truth wouldn't be so obvious to a person who has never been married before. In marriages of the widowed to never-married persons, the previously single mate must work hard to keep from developing an inferiority complex when the deceased mate is glorified in larger-than-life terms. It helps if the previously single partner is a stable, mature person with a strong sense of personal identity.

As you can see, the type of second-marriage union you are entering does have a bearing on the adjustments you can expect in your relationship. If you and your fiancé could talk about some of these possible problems *now*, *before* you are married, you might be able to defuse some of these dangerous land mines. Don't worry, there will be plenty of adjustments that neither of you anticipate. That's all the more reason for confronting the ones you can foresee well in advance of the wedding day.

Think of Remarriage as a Unique Experience

Another principle that can guide you safely on the road to remarriage is to try to think of it as a totally new and unique experience. Many people blunder into remarriage without taking the time to reflect on what it might be like. Too many expect their remarriage to be a carbon copy of their first relationship. You will be much better prepared for the realities of the situation if you try to think of a second marriage as an experience unlike anything you have known before.

In a first-time marriage, a husband and wife establish many familiar joint routines as a part of the natural process of getting to know each other better. They work out a system of shopping, child-rearing, money management, community involvement, relationships to in-laws, etc., that is comfortable for them.

But in a typical remarriage, both the husband and the wife have already established these familiar routines through a previous relationship. This means that you and your mate must be willing to change some of your comfortable ways of doing things until you find a system that works well for the two of you. Don't expect this to happen overnight. Unlearning old habits and changing familiar patterns of behavior will probably take a lot of time. The older you and your mate are, the harder it will be. Try to be patient with each other during this period of adjustment. Above all, keep the communication lines clear and maintain your sense of humor. Sometimes a hearty laugh can defuse a potential explosion more effectively than a rational discussion.

While old habits are a powerful force in a remarriage, they are no problem at all, when compared with the "ghosts" of former relationships. This is the factor that makes remarriage such a unique experience. Old relationships from the past have a way of forcing their way into your present marriage and making unreasonable demands, usually at the time when you're least prepared to cope with them.

Take Connie and David, for example. They had no way of knowing before they married that Connie's ex-husband would be such a pain. No sooner had they said "I do" than he began to make persistent and annoying phone calls at all hours of the day. Every time he came by to pick up the children for a weekend at his apartment, he badgered Connie with personal questions about her present relationship with David.

Later, when the children returned home, they always showed by their behavior that their father had spent most of the weekend trying to turn them against Connie and their new stepfather. Although they tried to present a united front as a couple against all this harassment, their patience soon began to wear a little thin.

No matter how much you may need to believe that your remarriage represents a "new beginning," don't allow yourself to fall for that delusion. You can never wipe the slate clean and start all over again as if the previous relationship never existed. Your former mate, your children, and your ex-in-laws (your children's grandparents, remember?) will always be there to remind you of your previous marriage. Remarriage is not so much a "beginning again" as another chapter in your life. Maybe you can cope with its unique demands a little better if you think of it this way even before you get around to saying "I do" the second time.

Probe Your Motives for Marrying Again

Another thing you can do to make sure you are thinking straight about remarriage is to analyze your motives for getting married again. None of us is so objective, of course, that he is always aware of the underlying motives that make him act as he does. No matter how pure and noble we claim our actions are, most of us act out of a mixture of good and bad motives most of the time. So recognize from the very beginning that getting down to your true motives for remarriage is a tough, elusive task.

Maybe the best you can do is to make yourself aware of a number of motives that could be influencing your decision to get married again. Parents, work associates, or close friends are often more aware of our true motives than we ourselves. If you're open to their advice and counsel, they may be able to give you some real insight into your behavior.

Time can also be an ally in helping you sort out your motives. Whatever you do, never make an impulsive decision to get married again. Give a relationship time to grow and develop before you rush to the altar. Otherwise, you may find that what you thought was genuine love was really nothing more than a neurotic need to be dependent or to feel loved and wanted.

People who get married within a few months following their divorce often fall into this category. Ralph is a textbook example of this principle at work. His male ego took a real beating when his wife asked for a divorce because of her attraction to another man. Suffering from a deep sense of rejection, Ralph set out to prove to himself as well as to others that he was still "man enough" to command the affection of a woman. And Janice just happened to be the first one he found when he started looking around.

Ralph and Janice were married within four months after a whirlwind courtship. This marriage doesn't have the strong foundation of a mutual respect between husband and wife. Ralph tells himself that he loves Janice, but he's actually more in love with himself and his need for support and reassurance. His object is not to share his life with Janice; he's using her as a human ego prop. This flimsy foundation will never support the weight of a lasting marriage relationship.

Then there are those people who marry again for financial security. This is a big temptation for women, especially, who find themselves in a financial bind following a divorce.

Joanne was anxious to break out of her suffocating marriage with Mike because of his temper tantrums and insane fits of jealousy. But she never dreamed how tough it would be on her own. Mike did make child-support payments to help out with household expenses, but Joanne found these didn't go very far toward feeding, clothing, and providing shelter for two growing children. She finally took a second job as a waitress to help pay some of the overdue bills.

Then, overworked and exhausted by two jobs, she began to feel trapped and boxed in—like a helpless victim on a treadmill with no way to get off. At that time in her life, Joanne would have said yes without a second thought to any man who offered a way of escape from her financial prison.

Men aren't above the financial motive, either, in their search for a suitable remarriage partner. These days, there are plenty of eligible women who have money or high-paying professional careers with a bright future. And there are also plenty of men who would like nothing better than a generous supply of cash to support their leisurely and indulgent way of life.

Financial security as a goal of marriage is worthy and appropriate. Freedom from money worries can set a couple free to concentrate on building a deep relationship. But an adequate financial base needs to be a joint objective that both busband and wife are working toward. A marriage founded on nothing but one partner's quest for a life of plenty through the other is flawed from the very beginning. One mate is using the other for his own selfish purpose.

15

This will lead sooner or later to the collapse of the relationship.

Still another unworthy motive for remarriage is the desire for revenge. "Marriage on the rebound" is the way our pop culture describes this phenomenon. It happens when a person gets married again in an attempt to hurt his or her mate from a previous relationship.

Bruce is a classic example of this strange pattern of behavior. For years he and Eleanor had been having problems in their marriage. But Bruce refused to take them seriously. Eleanor finally went to a marriage counselor herself while Bruce sat home watching television or continued his carousing with "the boys."

When Eleanor announced that she was filing for divorce, Bruce's feelings progressed quickly from shock to hurt to outrage to deep resentment and hate. One week after the divorce was finalized, he married a woman whom he had been seeing on the sly for several months. And he went to great lengths to make sure his former wife heard about the marriage. He would show Eleanor he didn't have to be married to her in order to be happy! Bruce's remarriage was motivated by his desire for revenge against his former wife.

After reading this list of sick and unhealthy motives, you may be skeptical about the whole business of remarriage. How can you be absolutely sure that you are getting married again for the right reason? And how can you be certain that your marriage partner is not acting out of an ulterior motive?

Remember what we said in the beginning about mixed motives? Most of our actions are determined by a combination of good and bad. Our need as human beings for acceptance, love, and ego support is one of the main reasons we choose to marry rather than remain single the rest of our lives. So it's all right to marry out of your need for love—as long as you accept your responsibility to give love in return.

But a totally neurotic motive for remarriage cuts only one way. The person is so wrapped up in his own needs that he uses his marriage partner to meet those needs with no thought of giving anything in return. No person is ready for remarriage unless he is just as concerned about his mate's happiness as he is about his own welfare. This *mutual obligation* aspect of marriage is the acid test.

As you think about remarriage, do you look forward to sharing your life at a deep, intimate level with another person? Do you still think of marriage as a total commitment of two people to each other for life, in spite of your unfortunate experience with marriage the first time around? Do you look forward to the adventure of getting to know your mate even better than you know him now? Have you worked through your negative feelings toward the mate from a previous marriage? If you can answer these questions with a positive, unqualified yes, then you shouldn't worry about your motives. If your fiancé feels as you do, then both of you are probably ready to give marriage another try.

These are some of the principles that should guide your thinking along the path toward remarriage. They may not be the most romantic place to begin your journey, but they are essential if you want to build a lasting and successful relationship the second time around. Now that you have done some hard-headed thinking about remarriage and its demands, move on to Chapter 2 for some important pointers on planning the wedding.

Notes

_____

_____

_____

_____

_____

_____

2
Planning the Wedding

Your initial impulse may tell you that getting ready for a second wedding is a simple task. After all, either you or your fiancé—or maybe both—have been through this before. Shouldn't all this valuable experience make second-wedding planning a breeze?

The answer is yes and no. You should have a better idea of the procedures involved in getting ready for this big event. But remember that second-time weddings are more than just a re-hash of what you did the first time around. The circumstances under which you are marrying are quite different. These call for some unique planning steps. Use the following points as a general guide to make sure you touch all the bases in getting ready for the wedding.

Let the Children in on Your Plans

The first order of business is to break the news to your children as well as to your fiancé's children that the two of you are planning to be married. And don't wait until a month or two before the wedding. Do this as soon as possible after you decide to take the plunge. Your children have a big stake in your future relationship as husband and wife, and they deserve to be informed about what lies ahead.

If your children have been subjected to the trauma of their parents' divorce, they particularly need to be informed as soon as possible about your plans for remarriage. Studies have shown that many children live under the delusion that their divorced parents might get together again. Sometimes they continue to believe this for years, even after their parents begin to date other people. You don't have to be a psychologist to figure out what a sudden announcement of remarriage plans can do to a child who is living with this myth. It shatters his illusion, and the natural reaction is to strike out negatively against the idea of remarriage.

If your child should react passively to the news about your remarriage, don't assume that he's handling it well. He could be hiding his secret fears and insecurities. A single parent and his or her children often develop a very close relationship. So your child may be thinking that he's losing his special place with you, now that you're taking on a wife or a husband. Or, he may be wondering exactly where he will fit in the scheme of things after all of you merge into one family.

Try to be sensitive to the moods and thoughts of your children during this time. Encourage them to talk openly about their fears and doubts. Don't allow them to veto your plans for marriage. But do permit them to air their reservations and negative feelings if they have any. Above all, talk and listen to each other. This can smooth the path toward remarriage and help assure that your wedding will be a happy experience for everyone in the family.

Decide on the Type of Wedding

Next on the agenda is deciding on the type of wedding you and your fiancé would like to have. You need to make this decision early in the planning process, since the type of wedding influences other factors such as date, type of ceremony, reception plans, etc.

If you want to avoid a lot of the hassle that elaborate weddings require, then a simple at-home ceremony may be for you. The two of you could pledge your vows to each other in the intimate atmosphere of one of your homes, with relatives and a few close friends in attendance.

One of the biggest arguments for an at-home wedding is the reasonable cost. Such frills as flowers, candles, multiple attendants, and an elaborate reception are usually eliminated. This allows you to hold the costs at a very reasonable level. In many second weddings the bride and groom share equally in the expenses. So don't be afraid to choose the smooth and simple at-home route if this suits your style and your budget.

On the other hand, don't rule out the possibility of an elaborate church wedding if finances are no problem and this is what the two of you really want. This type of wedding is particularly appropriate in situations where the groom has been married before but the bride is getting married for the first time. It's considered tasteful and proper for her to have a formal wedding with all the trimmings and for her parents to bear most of the expenses.

Even if the bride has been married before, you can still have a big church wedding if this is a high priority with one or both of you. Perhaps the bride got married in a simple civil ceremony the first time and she wants to make this wedding an occasion to remember. Or, it may be important to the groom to "take a wife" in a service that is really something special.

No matter what the etiquette books say, you can have a big second wedding if this is what you want. Just make sure you and your fiancé are in agreement about this approach.

Somewhere between a simple home wedding and an elaborate church wedding are a couple of other options you may want to consider. What about an outdoor wedding? Or a wedding in a small chapel at your church? Either of these is a good compromise if you want something a little nicer than a home wedding without spending a lot of money.

Suitable sites for outdoor weddings include gardens, parks, backyards, beaches, and college campuses. The nice thing about an outside location is that the flowers and greenery are provided by nature absolutely free. Your biggest headaches will be arranging seating for the guests and working out the details for recorded or live vocal and instrumental music. And don't forget the weather. Be sure to have a back-up plan in case it's raining when the hour for the big event arrives.

Many couples find a small chapel at their church is the ideal place for a second wedding. It will accommodate more guests than a home, but it's still small enough to provide a relaxed, informal setting in which they can pledge their vows. A chapel also requires few flowers and decorations, allowing considerable savings on wedding expenses.

So these are the four types of weddings you have to choose from: at home, outdoors, small chapel service, or elaborate church wedding. Talk these choices over with your fiancé to determine which is right for you. Be levelheaded and realistic about how you will share the expenses and how much money you can afford to spend.

Above all, get started early with your wedding plans. There's a lot more to planning a wedding than most couples realize, even if you have been through the experience before. This time around, you probably don't have as much time to give to wedding planning. An early start is your best assurance that you'll have everything ready when the big day arrives.

Confer With Your Minister

Another thing you should do early in your planning is to talk with the minister whom you want to officiate at the ceremony. Your first choice may be the minister of your own church. But make sure you are prepared mentally for this initial conference, particularly if you or your fiancé have been divorced.

Some ministers refuse to perform a ceremony for a couple with a broken marriage in their past. Don't get your hopes up before finding out your minister's stand on this issue.

Even if your minister won't perform the ceremony, he may have no problem with your scheduling the wedding at the church and enlisting another minister to officiate. You might be prepared to suggest this as an alternative, in case you meet with some resistance.

Suppose your church building can't be used for weddings by those who have been divorced? If you have your heart set on a church wedding, you have no choice but to find another house of worship that doesn't practice this kind of exclusion. If you look around, you should find some churches in your area that are a little more open on this matter.

You might also check with some of the leading florists in your city. In recent years flower shops and other firms that cater to the wedding business have established wedding chapels as a service to their customers. Most of these are furnished like the interior of a church building. You'll probably have to pay a fee for the use of one of these "bridal chapels," but t' do represent a good alternative for people who want to avoid the hassle of lining up a church.

Enlist the Wedding Party and Decide on Appropriate Dress

After deciding on the type of wedding you want, conferring with the minister and setting the date, you are ready to think about the people whom you want to be a part of the wedding party. How many attendants will the bride have? And who will serve as the groom's best man? These people need to be contacted and enlisted well in advance of the wedding day.

The rule of thumb here is to let the type of wedding you are planning and your unique remarriage circumstances be the guide in determining the size of the wedding party. If you have decided on a formal church wedding, for example, it's considered appropriate—though not mandatory—for the bride to have several additional attendants as well as a bridesmaid. But if you have opted for a small, intimate wedding in the chapel of a church, you might prefer to have no attendants at all. The bride and groom could walk down the aisle together and join the minister at the altar.

Still other couples getting married for the second time decide on two attendants—a bridesmaid for the bride and a best man for the groom. Use your own judgment in deciding on what pattern is best for you and the type of wedding you are planning. As a general rule, the more lavish the wedding, the larger the wedding party should be.

After deciding on the size of the wedding party and enlisting the people, you face the question of appropriate dress for this group in a second wedding. Just as in a first-time wedding, the bride sets the pace for the others.

Good taste dictates that a woman who has been married before should not wear a long, traditional white wedding dress or a veil. These make her look too much like a first-time bride. But many second-time brides these days are wearing a very dressy long or short white dress and a delicate hat with a hint of a veil. Some, of course, avoid white altogether and choose off-white, beige, or ivory as the scheme for their wedding dress.

22

The point is that second-time brides exercise more freedom today in deciding what to wear at their weddings. The one solid rule you shouldn't violate is: *Avoid the look of a first-time bride.*

Bridal consultants offer these suggestions to second-time brides to help them look their very best on their wedding day.

• Consider wearing a bridesmaid's dress. They are dressy and feminine, but they don't make you look like a first-time bride.

• Avoid an all-lace wedding dress with a high neck and long sleeves. This is practically guaranteed to give you the look you want to avoid. You'll find that a lace suit or short-sleeve dress is much more appropriate for the occasion.

• If you do choose a dress of pure white, be sure to tone it down with a dash of color. This contrasting color could appear in your purse or a jacket, for example.

The bride's attendant should follow her lead in the type of wedding dress she selects. For example, if the bride wears a dressy short dress, her attendant should wear a similar dress that coordinates well with the bride's outfit. In some second weddings, the bride's teenage daughter may serve as her mother's attendant. In this situation remember that it will look much more appropriate for her to wear a prom dress or a fancy party dress than a more formal bridesmaid's outfit. It's more important for her to look like the daughter than to fill the formal role of an adult attendant.

Younger daughters of the bride and groom involved in the wedding should wear their "Sunday best." Boys who are male attendants or ushers should follow the lead of the groom in the way they dress. The same principle holds true for adult males who serve as ushers or groomsmen in the wedding.

As far as clothes for the groom himself, he should dress in a manner that fits the formality of the wedding—formal wear for a formal event or a dark, solid suit for informal and semiformal weddings.

The parents of the bride and groom should also follow the principle of dressing to suit the formality of the occasion. In most second weddings, the parents have no special role to fill other than being present for the marriage of their son or daughter. The one exception to this might be a wedding where the father gives his daughter away, if she is getting married for the first time to a man who has been married before. In a case like this where the wedding is very formal, the bride's father might elect to dress formally as a member of the wedding party.

On all questions of appropriate dress for a second wedding, don't hesitate to contact a formal wear agency or a bridal consultant. They deal with these questions routinely as a part of their business and can help you make decisions on the right dress for all members of the wedding party.

Decide on Invitations and Announcements

Another important element in wedding planning is making appropriate announcements about your marriage and ordering the invitations after you decide on the guest list and the procedure for inviting guests. Here again, second weddings have some unique angles that must be considered.

To begin with, most couples getting married again don't make such a big deal out of their engagement as they did the first time around. So you may want to skip the procedure of sending a formal announcement to your local newspaper, unless this is a first-time marriage for the bride. Many newspapers by policy don't publish remarriage announcements.

The question of whom to invite to a second wedding can became very sticky unless you use your common sense and talk out your feelings thoroughly with your fiancé. Very seldom would it be appropriate to invite an ex-spouse to the wedding, for example, but beyond that the waters get very murky. No wonder many couples getting married again keep their weddings small and informal. This automatically limits the guest list, avoiding some of the thorny questions about whom to invite.

What about your ex-in-laws? If you have children, you have probably retained a close tie to them because of their relationship with their grandchildren. But would their presence at the wedding bring back too many unhappy memories and mar the happiness of this occasion? Would they feel uncomfortable at a wedding where their ex-daughter-in-law or ex-son-in-law is marrying again?

These are some of the questions you need to consider as you try to decide whether to invite relatives from a previous relationship to the wedding. Don't invite those whose presence would be embarrassing either for them or to you.

One possibility to consider is a small wedding with a restricted guest list, followed by a reception to which you invite a larger number, including all ex-relatives from previous relationships. This allows you to include these people in the wedding festivities without subjecting anyone to morbid memories from the past.

How should invitations to a second wedding be issued? And what form should they take? There's no one easy answer to either of these questions. It depends on a number of factors, including whether the wedding is formal or informal, how much the couple wants to spend on invitations, and whether the bride's parents are giving the wedding or most of the planning has been done by the couple themselves.

All the possible types of invitations to a second wedding can be grouped for convenience into three categories: (1) Informal handwritten invitations to the wedding, written by the bride, (2) printed invitations to the wedding, issued by the bride and groom, and (3) formal, engraved invitations to the wedding, issued in the name of relatives of the bride.

Here are several examples of invitations from each of these categories. They should guide you in deciding on the invitation approach and pattern that is best for your wedding:

Examples of Informal, Handwritten Invitations to the Wedding, Written by the Bride

Dear Mike and Jennifer,

Jim and I are getting married Saturday, September 20, and we hope you can join us for this happy occasion. The wedding is scheduled for 4:00 P.M. at my home, 2148 Ridgebrook, in the Castle Hills subdivision. We hope you can also join us for the brief reception to follow.

Love,
Penny

Dear Aunt Laura,

Edward and I hope you can join us on Saturday, June 11, when we pledge our vows to each other as husband and wife. The wedding is scheduled for 4:00 P.M in the chapel at Forest Hills United Methodist Church, 2100 Belmont Boulevard, Akron, Ohio, with a brief reception to follow in the church's fellowship hall.

Love,
Beth

Dear Ralph and Sandra,

Dan and I plan to be married "under the stars" in the beautiful rose garden in Central Park on Friday evening, August 10, at 7:00 P.M. We hope you can join us for the celebration. In case of rain, the ceremony will take place under picnic shelter #5 directly across the street from the rose garden.

Love,
Marie

Examples of Printed Invitations to the Wedding, Issued by the Bride and Groom

A Wedding Celebration
Please join us for our wedding
and for refreshments afterward
Doris Marie Morgan and Gregory A. Campbell
September 19
4:00 o'clock
2148 Ridgebrook Drive
Charlotte, North Carolina

The honor of your presence
is requested at the marriage of
Susan Faye Warrington
and
Douglas Stephen Smith, Jr.
on Saturday, November 11, at four o'clock
First United Church of Christ
1015 Main Street
Portland, Oregon

DEBORAH CAROL TAYLOR and JOHN WARREN MOORE
The special day of our marriage is
February 21, at 8:00 P.M.
St. James Episcopal Church
1028 Coledonia Avenue, Murfreesboro, Tennessee
We hope you will join us for this happy occasion
and celebrate with us after the ceremony
at the Hillwood Village Clubhouse

With Christian joy
Karen Diane Oliver
and
Louie Martin Craig
invite you to worship and celebrate
as they unite their lives in holy matrimony
on Saturday the tenth of December
at half past three
Bryan Memorial Presbyterian Church
4816 Greentree Drive
Lexington, Kentucky

We invite you to be with us
as we begin our new life together
on Saturday, March tenth,
at three o'clock
University Baptist Church
1423 Memorial Drive
Austin, Texas
If you are unable to attend,
we ask your presence in thought and prayer
Virginia Crawford
and
Carl Wagner

Examples of Formal, Engraved Invitations to the Wedding, Issued in the Names of Relatives of the Bride

Mr. and Mrs. John Paul Jenkins
invite you to share in the joy
of seeing their daughter
Jennifer Sue
united with
Robert Wayne Bollinger
on Saturday, July fourteenth
at six o'clock
Redeemer Lutheran Church
6213 East Iowa Avenue
Green Bay, Wisconsin

With thanksgiving to God
who has prepared
Janice Loraine Evans
and
Mark Allman Brooks
to be united in marriage,
we,
Mr. and Mrs. Richard C. Evans
invite you to worship with us, witness their vows,
and share in their love for one another
on Saturday, the eighteenth of June,
at two o'clock in the afternoon
St. Cecilia Catholic Church
Sedalia, Missouri

Mr. Donald Etheridge
requests the pleasure of your company
at the marriage of his daughter
Karla Ann Duncan
to
William Ray Cunningham
on Saturday, September the second,
at two o'clock
Church of the Covenant
1015 Golden Street
Phoenix, Arizona

To order printed or engraved invitations, check with a print shop that specializes in this type of printing. Some printers, gift shops, and stationery stores also offer a wide range of blank stock for those who prefer to issue their own handwritten invitations.

Take Care of Miscellaneous Wedding Details

After you think you've completed all the planning for a wedding, a lot of little extraneous details have a way of popping up. For example, what should you do if a well-meaning friend offers to give you a shower? Most etiquette experts agree that gifts for a second wedding should be discouraged. After all, at least one of you has been married before, so you already have a lot of the essentials for setting up housekeeping. The best approach is to discourage showers and other gift-giving events.

Of course, if gifts arrive in connection with the wedding and some of your friends plan a secret shower, there's little you can do but accept graciously. And don't forget to have thank-you note cards handy, just in case.

Such customs as the bridal luncheon, the bachelor party, and the rehearsal dinner are also considered inappropriate for second weddings. Even the after-wedding reception is seldom the big "bash" most people have come to expect in connection with first-time weddings. And this is probably a good thing for you and your fiancé. Since you're probably paying the bills this time, just think what all these festivities together would cost. The two of you will have enough adjustments to make without worrying about paying off a big wedding debt.

One social event you might consider that won't cost a fortune is to invite the wedding party to your home or a nice restaurant for dinner as soon as you are settled. What better way to start your life together as husband and wife than sharing some of the special memories of your wedding with a few close friends? This is a beautiful way to say thank-you to some of the special people in your lives.

* * *

Now that you have done some important preliminary planning for your wedding, you are ready to think about the ceremony for this occasion. The next three chapters are designed to help you arrange and select an appropriate service for a second wedding.

3
Making the Ceremony Simple but Special

The heart of any wedding is the ceremony, with the vows and promises that you and your mate make to each other as husband and wife. As a general rule, first-time weddings are more elaborate, containing such frills as vocal and instrumental music, multiple attendants, and other elaborate details. Good taste dictates that a remarriage ceremony should be simpler and more refined in its approach.

After all, this is the second time that you and your fiancé have been through such a ceremony. You don't have to impress people with a big production like you did the first time around. Remember, too, that the two of you are probably sharing the expenses for this wedding. It's amazing how this sobering truth can help you scale down your wedding plans!

But make sure you don't push the "no frills" ceremony approach a little too far. It is possible to make your remarriage service so basic and plain that it comes across more like a funeral than a wedding. *Simple but special* is the balance you need to strive for. Here are some guidelines to help you achieve this magic formula with your ceremony.

Be Aware of Second Wedding Taboos

Second weddings are subject to several unique matters of etiquette—let's call them taboos—that you are probably well aware of

31

by now. Perhaps the strongest is that a woman who has been married before should not wear white at her wedding, since the pure-white bridal gown signifies purity and virginity.

Most previously-married women bow to this taboo by wearing ivory or off-white at their second wedding. To avoid the "blushing bride" syndrome, they usually wear a dressy but tasteful long or street-length dress. The bridal train and veil are generally considered inappropriate also for second-time brides.

This taboo does not apply, of course, when a never-married woman becomes the bride of a man who has been married before. In this case, she may dress as she wishes without breaking any social customs. When the situation is reversed—previously-married woman marrying a never-married man—some women ignore custom and dress like a first-time bride because this is important to the groom. Only you can be the judge of when to follow this social taboo and when to do your own thing. Feel free to bend the rules when you have good reason for it.

Another taboo about second weddings is that a previously-married woman should never be "given away" again by her father—or any other man, for that matter. The reasoning behind this is that she has already been initiated into the adult world where she has become her own person. It would look a little ridiculous to go through another "giving away" ritual.

In most second weddings, the bride simply walks down the aisle without a male escort and joins the groom at the altar. The part about "Who gives this woman . . ." is eliminated from the service. Another alternative is for the bride and groom to walk down the aisle together and join the minister at the altar. This is particularly appropriate at simple ceremonies where the bride has no attendants and the groom has no best man.

Sometimes a bride with sons wonders about letting them serve as stand-ins for her father during this part of the ceremony. If you want to be "given away" by your sons, that's your prerogative, of course. But another approach is to let them serve as your escorts and then stand to the side looking on during the rest of the ceremony. This gives them an important part in the wedding without placing them in the role of authoritative parents.

Include the Children in the Ceremony

While we're on the subject of children, let's nail down another principle for planning a simple but special ceremony: Look for ways to include children of both the bride and the groom at appropriate places in the ceremony. This assumes, of course, that your children want to be involved and that they're old enough to carry out their ceremony responsibilities.

Young children might serve as flower girls or the ring bearer. Older children could fill many additional roles, including escorts, ushers, best men, attendants, or groomsmen.

Give the Ceremony Your Own Personal Touch

Another way to keep your ceremony simple but to make it special at the same time is to give it your own personal touch. This could mean writing your own vows and repeating them to each other at the appropriate place in the service. Or, you and your fiancé might select a piece of vocal music that has particular meaning for you and enlist someone to sing it at just the right moment during the ceremony. The possibilities for creative personal touches like this are endless. More and more couples, even in second weddings, are customizing their ceremonies to make them unique and memorable.

If you would like to add some innovative personal touches to your ceremony, be sure to check first with the officiating minister. Make sure he is open to the idea of using elements of your creation in the wedding service. He may have a standard ceremony that he prefers to use in all the weddings he conducts. You might assure him that you and your fiancé plan to do all the work of arranging a new wedding service. Give him your assurance that he can check the ceremony after you've completed it to make sure he has no objection to the content.

Most ministers don't object to the bride and groom arranging their own ceremony, as long as they are consulted early in the planning process. Besides, he might have some additional resources and ideas from other weddings that you can use in working out your own personal touch.

One good rule to remember as you add innovative touches to the wedding service is the principle of balance. Try to balance every new and creative element with some traditional approach that will be recognized instantly by your wedding guests. Otherwise, you may end up with a ceremony so modern and radical that it comes across as cold and unfeeling. Remember that most people find comfort and security in the familiar. Your goal should be to strike a balance between the traditional and the contemporary as you plan the ceremony.

Consider the Different Elements of a Wedding Ceremony

Before you can plan those unique personal touches for your own wedding, you need to review the different elements that are usually included in a Christian wedding ceremony. Here's a quick recap of the major features.

Music. Appropriate music is one of the key ingredients of a memorable wedding. There should be no background music during the parts of the ceremony when people are speaking, since this only detracts from the beauty and solemnity of the occasion. But music of the following four distinct types at special times during the wedding lends its own unique beauty.

1. *Prelude.* Quiet instrumental music by the organist or pianist is appropriate while guests are being seated before the service begins. A medley of well-known hymns is always appropriate in a church wedding. In some weddings vocal music may be included as part of the prelude just before the wedding party enters the church.

2. *Processional.* The tempo of the music always picks up when the wedding party enters the church. Hymn singing by the congregation during the processional seems to be gaining in popularity in many weddings.

3. *Recessional.* Lovely instrumental music while the wedding party leaves the church at the end of the service is a standard feature of most contemporary church weddings. Joyous and exuberant hymns of praise are appropriate during the recessional.

4. *Vocal Music.* Vocal solos or duets at one or two places during the ceremony lend a special dignity to many church weddings. One of the most popular selections is "The Lord's Prayer," often sung by a soloist as the couple kneel in prayer following their vows or the exchange of rings. Some popular songs may also be appropriate if their lyrics have an underlying Christian message.

34

Opening Words of the Minister. The introductory statement of the minister usually consists of a short summary of the meaning of marriage as revealed in the Bible. Some words are generally included about the significance of the ceremony that is about to take place.

Prayers of the Minister. Every Christian wedding ceremony should include at least one or two prayers for God's guidance and direction in your lives. Prayers of thanksgiving are also in order. Usually these prayers are led by the officiating minister.

Scripture Passages. One or two passages of Scripture on the meaning of marriage are generally included in a Christian wedding. These are usually read by the minister.

Congregational Responses. Participation in the wedding by the guests is a high priority with many couples getting married for either the first or second time. They want their guests to enter into the celebration of this occasion rather than just sit and watch as passive spectators.

One good way to get your guests involved is to include a congregational response in your ceremony. This usually takes the form of a litany of praise, with the minister making certain statements about the goodness of God and the congregation responding in unison with their own words of praise. If you include a feature like this in your wedding, you'll need to provide a printed worship bulletin with all these responsive elements printed in full.

Exchange of Vows. The heart of the Christian wedding ceremony is the exchange of vows between bride and groom. More and more couples today are writing their own vows and saying them to each other rather than repeating prescribed "formula vows" under the direction of the officiating minister.

If you write your own vows, be sure to keep them brief—no more than four or five sentences long. This is not the place for long, rambling essays on the nature and philosophy of marriage. Your vows should be intimate and personal. Remember, you are making promises to each other—not to the wedding guests or to the rest of the wedding party.

Exchange of Rings. The purpose of the exchange of rings is to seal or symbolize the pledges of devotion which you and your mate have made to each other. So this part of the ceremony always comes logically right after the exchange of vows.

Just before the exchange of rings, the minister usually makes some statement about the symbolism of the rings. This statement could be made just as easily by both of you as you slip the rings on each other's fingers. The trend in the double ring ceremony nowadays seems to be toward a simple and direct ring exchange. The bride and groom may say to each other, "I give you this ring as a symbol of my devotion. Wear it to show others that you are touched by my love."

Lighting of the Unity Candle. In recent years more and more Christian couples have been including a custom called the lighting of the unity candle in their wedding ceremonies. This always occurs near the end of the service. The bride and groom each take a lighted candle and light a larger candle to symbolize the union of their lives in marriage.

If you include this element in your ceremony, you might decide to make some statement as husband and wife about the marriage union which has just been formed. Or, the minister might read some appropriate Scripture, such as Genesis 2:23-24, about "two becoming one," as you and your mate light the unity candle.

Declaration of Marriage and Final Charge by the Minister. This is a formal statement by the minister that the bride and groom are now united as husband and wife. This declaration is often combined with a concluding prayer or charge to the couple to work together to build a Christian home. Other brief comments from the minister about the holiness and permanence of marriage are also appropriate.

This review gives you a quick introduction to the elements that are usually included in a wedding ceremony. Now move on to Chapter 4 for a look at some sample ingredients from other services that are particularly appropriate for second weddings.

4
Ingredients
for Remarriage Ceremonies
From Other Weddings

The previous chapter gave you a quick review of the typical elements in a Christian wedding ceremony. Now you need to take a look at what some other couples have done to give these elements their own personal touch. The following sample ingredients from other ceremonies have been selected because they are particularly appropriate for second weddings. Read these over carefully with your fiancé and select the ones that appeal to you. This should put you in tune with each other about the personal touches you would like to include in your own wedding service.

MUSIC FOR THE WEDDING

Prelude (while the wedding guests are being seated)

"Jesu, Joy of Man's Desiring"
"Ode to Joy"
"Praise to the Lord the Almighty"
"Awake, My Heart, With Gladness"
"Love's Greeting"
"Invocation"

Processional (while the wedding party enters the church)

"Praise Ye the Father"
"Trumpet Tune in D Major"
"Festival March"
"Joyful, Joyful, We Adore Thee"
"Processional on Westminster Abbey"

Vocal Music (during the ceremony)

"The Greatest of These Is Love"
"Both Sides Now"
"We've Only Just Begun"
"The Lord's Prayer"
"Here at Thine Altar, Lord"
"O Perfect Love"
"Wedding Song"
"Though I Speak With the Tongues"
"Our Wedding Prayer"
"Thou Wilt Keep Him in Perfect Peace"
"I Love You Truly"
"O Promise Me"
"My Heart Ever Faithful"
"O Lord Most Holy"

Organ Music (during the ceremony)

"Blest Be the Tie That Binds"
"O Jesus, I Have Promised"
"O Love That Will Not Let Me Go"
"A Joyous March"
"Trumpet Voluntary"

Congregational Hymns (during the ceremony)

"Love Divine, All Loves Excelling"
"Saviour, Like a Shepherd Lead Us"
"Pass It On"

"For the Beauty of the Earth"
"Be Thou My Vision"
"All Creatures of Our God and King"
"Sweet, Sweet Spirit"

Recessional (while the wedding party leaves the church)

"Doxology"
"Theme From the Masterpiece Theater"
"In Thee Is Gladness"
"Now Thank We All Our God"
"Wedding March From Midsummer Night's Dream"
"Hymn to Joy"
"Fanfare"
"O God, Our Help in Ages Past"

OPENING WORDS OF THE MINISTER

Life's Most Sacred Relationship

We have met here today to witness the union of this couple in life's most sacred relationship. Edwin and Barbara, your relationship as husband and wife will be so close and intimate that it will profoundly influence your whole future. As you stand here today, you cannot possibly foresee how pleasure and pain will be interminged in your future. But it is a great tribute to your faith in each other that you are willing to face these uncertainties together. May the love with which you join your hearts and hands today never fail but grow deeper and stronger with every year you spend together.

The Center of God's Will

We, as a community of friends and loved ones, are gathered here today to celebrate the marriage of Daniel and Kathryn and to ask God to bless them in this union. We are called to rejoice in their happiness, to support them when they have difficulties, and to hold them up in our prayers. It is God's clear intention that a husband and wife should love each other throughout their life and provide an atmosphere of security and stability for their children.

Daniel and Kathryn, your marriage should join you for the rest of your days in a relationship so deep and caring that it will change your whole being. God promises that he will honor and deepen your love if you will keep your relationship in the center of his will.

God's Intention for Marriage

We are gathered here today in the sight of God and in the presence of this company to witness the union of Joyce Marie Cunningham and William Roy Powell in Christian marriage. May our Heavenly Father look down upon this special day with his smile of approval. May our Lord Jesus Christ be present and add his blessing. May the Holy Spirit attend and seal these vows in love. For marriage is a precious gift from God himself—given to promote social order and to increase human happiness.

When God created man and placed him in the Garden of Eden, he saw immediately that it was not good for man to live alone. So he prepared for him a helper and companion and presented her to man. This shows us very clearly that marriage is God's good gift to deliver us from our loneliness and isolation. This is why the book of Genesis declares, "Therefore shall a man leave his father and his mother, and shall cleave unto his wife: and they shall be one flesh" (Gen. 2:25). This is the type of union that William and Joyce desire as they stand before us today.

PRAYERS OF THE MINISTER

Prayer for a Mature Love

Our gracious Lord, we ask for Richard and Karen a full life—a life rich in meaning, purpose, and joy. We ask not that they be "happy ever after," although we hope their joys will be many in their new relationship as husband and wife. We ask, rather, that they have the grace and determination to work at building a mature love and mutual respect for each other—a love that will be strong enough to keep on loving through all the circumstances of life. Through Jesus Christ our Lord. Amen.

Prayer for Love and Joy

Eternal Father, apart from you no promise or vow is sure. We ask you to guide Robert and Elaine on their journey as they begin their pilgrimage of marriage together. Remind them always of the promises they have made to each other today. Fill them with such love and joy that they will build a home where no one is a stranger. And teach them through your word to practice gentleness and kindness in their relationship as husband and wife. In Jesus' name. Amen.

Prayer of Thanksgiving

O God, Creator and Father of us all, we thank you for the gift of marriage. We praise you for all the joys that come to us through marriage, and for the blessings of home and family. Today, especially, we think of Mike and Susan as they begin their married life together. Thank you for the happiness they have found in each other. Give them grace and strength to fulfill the vows they have made. Help them to cherish the love they share, that they may be faithful and devoted to each other forever. Enrich their love with patience, understanding, honesty, and wisdom so they may establish a home that is dedicated to you and your will for their lives. Through Jesus Christ our Lord. Amen.

SCRIPTURE PASSAGES

Any of the following passages of Scripture would be appropriate for a second wedding ceremony. The minister could read one or two of the passages near the beginning of the service. Be sure to check the verses in several different translations of the Bible to see which version you prefer. Short excerpts from several of these passages could be woven together to form a creative and unusual reading.

- Genesis 1:26-27: Creation of Man
- Genesis 2:18, 21-24: Creation of Woman
- Genesis 24:48-51, 58-67: Marriage of Isaac and Rebekah
- Ruth 1:16-17: "Entreat me not to leave thee . . ."
- Psalm 29:1-2: "Give unto the Lord glory . . ."
- Psalm 34:3: "O magnify the Lord with me . . ."
- Psalm 63:1-4: "O God, thou art my God . . ."
- Psalm 95:1-6: "O come, let us sing unto the Lord . . ."
- Psalm 100: "Make a joyful noise unto the Lord . . ."
- Psalm 127: "Except the Lord build the house . . ."
- Psalm 150: "Praise God in his sanctuary . . ."

- Proverbs 18:22: "Whoso findeth a wife . . ."
- Proverbs 24:3-4: Foundation of a Home
- Proverbs 31: 10-31: "Who can find a virtuous woman?"
- Ecclesiastes 4:9-12: "Two are better than one . . ."
- Song of Solomon 2:11-13: "For, lo, the winter is past . . ."
- Song of Solomon 5:16: "This is my beloved, and this is my friend . . ."
- Song of Solomon 6:3: "I am my beloved's . . ."
- Song of Solomon 8:6-7: "Set me as a seal . . ."
- Isaiah 61:10: "I will greatly rejoice in the Lord . . ."
- Jeremiah 33:11: "The voice of joy, and the voice of gladness . . ."
- Matthew 5:3-11: The Beatitudes
- Matthew 19:4-6: Christ's Statement on Marriage
- John 2:1-11: Christ at the Marriage in Cana
- John 15:9-17: Christ's Command to Love
- Romans 8:35-39: Our Assurance of God's Eternal Love
- 1 Corinthians 7:1-7: Marital Duties of Husbands and Wives
- 1 Corinthians 13: The Nature of Love
- Ephesians 5:21-33: Roles of Husbands and Wives
- Philippians 2:5-11: Proper Attitudes for Marriage
- Colossians 3:12-14: Forgiveness Essential in Marriage
- 1 Peter 3:1-7: Teachings for Husbands and Wives
- 1 John 3:16; 4:7-19: Teachings on Love

CONGREGATIONAL RESPONSES

Celebration of Creation

MINISTER: In the beginning God created the heavens and the earth.

CONGREGATION: And God said, Let us make man in our image, after our likeness.

MINISTER: And let them have dominion over the fish of the sea and over the fowl of the air, and over cattle.

CONGREGATION: And over all the earth and over every creeping thing that creepeth upon the earth.

MINISTER:	So God created man in his own image; in the image of God created he them.
CONGREGATION:	And God blessed them, and God said unto them, Be fruitful, and multiply and replenish the earth.
UNISON:	And God saw everything that he had made, and behold, it was very good, and the evening and the morning were the sixth day.

We Pledge Our Support

MINISTER:	This couple, Frank and Darlene, asks our blessing and friendship as they begin the adventure of married life as husband and wife.
CONGREGATION:	We pledge to support them in their task of building a deep and and abiding love.
MINISTER:	We realize that genuine love is not easily achieved. They will need determination and patience to renew their vows year after year in their pursuit of a lasting, loving relationship.
CONGREGATION:	We promise to help them in every appropriate way as they work at this task in their marriage.
MINISTER:	We recognize also that genuine love is fulfilled only as it reaches out to others. We ask that the unique love which Frank and Darlene feel for each other might reach out beyond themselves to their family, their friends, and the larger world in which they live.
CONGREGATION:	We promise to return this love as it reaches out to us. And we, in turn, will pass their love on to the larger universe in which we live.

We Have Come to Express Our Love

MINISTER:	We have gathered here today to share in the marriage celebration of Ralph and Janice. We rejoice that they have come to this point of commitment after cultivating their love for each other. We support their decision and their right to join together as husband and wife.

43

CONGREGATION:	As their friends and loved ones, we have come to help them celebrate this great moment in their lives.
MINISTER:	As a community of believers and friends, we pledge our support to Ralph and Janice as they begin their life together as a married couple. We pledge to open our community of fellowship to them and support them in their new roles as husband and wife.
CONGREGATION:	We have come today to express our love for Ralph and Janice and to wish them happiness for the future.

EXCHANGE OF VOWS

My Beloved and My Friend

(Directed by the bride to the groom as they hold hands and face each other.)

Jim, I promise to encourage you, pray for you, and always seek to be a helper and companion. I promise to work toward openness in our relationship, witholding nothing, and sharing fully with you my innermost thoughts. In my love for you, I will try to be patient and kind—not jealous, boastful, arrogant, or rude. I will not insist on my own way or be irritable or resentful. I will cultivate a love that keeps no record of your wrongs but always rejoices in the truth. Throughout our life together, I promise to cherish and honor you as my beloved and my friend.

Not Human Affection Alone

(Directed by the groom to the bride as they hold hands and face each other.)

Donna, God has been cultivating in us for many months a growing love. This love is rooted in something much more secure and stable than mere human affection. Behind it all is a strong, abiding sense of God's purpose for our lives. Recognizing this truth, I promise you as well as the Heavenly Father that I will strive to love you as Christ loved the church. Through all the days of our lives, I promise to remain true to you—in plenty and in want, in sickness and in health, in failure as well as in success. I give myself willingly to you and promise to make our home a haven of love and acceptance that will bring honor and glory to Christ.

Faith, Hope, and Joy

(In these vows, the bride and groom follow the leading of the minister as they repeat their promises to each other.)

MINISTER:	Don and Patricia, having felt the joy which accompanies your love for one another, and firmly believing in the fulfillment of a lifetime together, do you take each other to be husband and wife?
GROOM:	I, Don, take you, Patricia, as my wife.
BRIDE:	I, Patricia, take you, Don, as my husband.
MINISTER:	Do you both promise to bring faith, hope, and joy to your marriage?
GROOM:	I promise to bring faith, hope, and joy to our marriage.
BRIDE:	I promise to bring faith, hope, and joy to our marriage.
MINISTER:	Will you both be consoling, understanding, and forgiving?
GROOM:	I will be consoling, understanding, and forgiving.
BRIDE:	I will be consoling, understanding, and forgiving.
MINISTER:	Will you love each other and give yourselves fully to each other as husband and wife?
GROOM:	Patricia, I will love you and give myself fully to you as your husband.
BRIDE:	Don, I will love you and give myself fully to you as your wife.

Vows in Dialogue Form

(The bride and groom repeat the following vows in dialogue form as they hold hands and face each other.)

GROOM:	This is a day of celebration.

BRIDE:	Let us celebrate the goodness of God's love and the joy of human love.
GROOM:	On this special day, Anita, I pledge to love you forever. And I promise to respect your wishes and opinions in our marriage.
BRIDE:	Because I love you, Charles, I promise to make our marriage the most important thing in my life.
GROOM:	I will share with you my material goods as well as my deepest thoughts and feelings.
BRIDE:	And I will honor, cherish, and love you through all the days of our life.
GROOM:	I promise to help you grow as a person and to become everything you are capable of becoming.
BRIDE:	And I will support and encourage you through all the circumstances of life.
UNISON:	This is the first of many days together. Let us rejoice in the wonder of love.

EXCHANGE OF RINGS

Place the Ring . . . and Repeat After Me

(*The following is the longer version of the traditional double ring ceremony, with most of the talking done by the minister.*)

The perfect circle of a ring symbolizes eternity. God is the symbol of all that is pure and holy. Our prayer is that your love for each will be as eternal and everlasting as these rings. In the years to come these rings should remind you of the overwhelming joy of this special occasion when you were united in marriage. Karla (Steve), do you give this ring to Steve (Karla) as a token of your love for him (her)? (The bride (groom) should respond, "I do.") Then place the ring on his (her) finger and repeat after me:

I, Karla (Steve) take thee, Steve (Karla),

To be my wedded husband (wife),

To have and to hold from this day forward;

For better, for worse,

For richer, for poorer,

In sickness and in health;
To love and to cherish 'til death do us part,
According to God's holy ordinance—
And with this ring I pledge thee my love.

A Sign to All

GROOM: With this ring I symbolize our union—for to-day, tomorrow, and all the years to come. Please wear it as a sign to all that you have chosen me to be your husband.

BRIDE: With this ring I also symbolize our union—for today, tomorrow, and all the years to come. Please wear it as a sign to all that you have chosen me to be your wife.

I Accept You

GROOM: With this ring I thee wed. I accept you as my wife and joyfully proclaim it to all the world. I acknowledge you as my life partner, my belov-ed, and my friend.

BRIDE: With this ring I thee wed. I accept you as my husband and joyfully proclaim it to all the world. I acknowledge you as my life partner, my beloved, and my friend.

I Give You This Ring

(*Many couples are using a shorter version of the exchange of rings, making a simple statement about the significance of the rings as they place them on each other's finger. Any of the following short declarations are appropriate for a remarriage ceremony.*)

- "With all my love I give you this ring—an everlasting symbol of the vows we have made to each other today."
- "Jonathan (Kathy), I offer you this ring as a symbol of my en-during love and commitment. I ask that you wear it to show others you are touched by my love."
- "This ring I offer to you as a symbol of my love and faith-fulness."

- "Monica (James), take this ring and wear it as a symbol of our marriage vows and of our undying love for each other."

LIGHTING OF THE UNITY CANDLE

No Longer Two but One

(Spoken by the minister as the bride and groom each take a candle and light one central candle together.)

God's will for marriage is that the man shall leave his family and the woman shall leave her home and the two of them shall be united as one in a new relationship as husband and wife. Roger and Sherry will now proclaim their union as they individually light the central candle to symbolize their relationship. "So they are no longer two but one," Jesus declared. "What therefore God has joined together, let no man put asunder" (Matt. 19:6, RSV).

Union and Identity

(Spoken by the minister as the couple light the unity candle but leave their own separate candles burning.)

Marriage brings two people into a unique relationship. In their union they share many experiences as if they were one person. But each member of this relationship also retains his own identity. Genuine love allows us to overcome our sense of loneliness and isolation, yet permits us our uniqueness as individuals. The beautiful paradox of Christian marriage is that two people become as one (bride and groom light the unity candle), and yet they remain as two individuals (bride and groom place their individual candles, still burning, on the altar), created in the image of God.

DECLARATION OF MARRIAGE AND FINAL CHARGE BY THE MINISTER

Grant You Length of Days

Ernie and Dianne, since you have pledged your mutual vows to each other, it is now my pleasure as a minister of the gospel to pronounce you husband and wife. What God has joined together let no one put asunder. Would you kneel together as we pray?

May the Lord grant you length of days, vigor of body, deep and abiding mutual understanding, companionship, and love. And may this love grow stronger and stronger with the passing years. Now the Lord bless you and keep you; the Lord make his face to shine upon you, and be gracious unto you; the Lord lift up his countenance upon you and give you peace, both now and forever-more. Through Jesus Christ our Lord. Amen.

Establish and Sustain You

Since Jason and Margaret have consented together in holy matrimony before God and these friends, and have exchanged vows and rings, I now pronounce that they are husband and wife, in accordance with God's holy ordinance. Let no one divide these two whom God has brought together. Now (directing his remarks to the couple), the Lord God who created the first couple and established them in marriage, establish and sustain you, that you may find delight in each other and grow in holy love as long as you both shall live. Let us pray.

Eternal God, creator and preserver of all of life, look with favor upon these your servants, Jason and Margaret, who have pledged their lives to each other here today. Grant that they may live according to your will, with peace, joy, and love. Make their life together a reflection of your love and eternal grace. Now hear us as we pray together the Model Prayer our Lord taught us to pray, saying:

Our Father, who art in heaven, hallowed be thy name. Thy kingdom come, thy will be done, on earth as it is in heaven. Give us this day our daily bread. And forgive us our debts, as we forgive our debtors. And lead us not into temptation, but deliver us from evil. For thine is the kingdom, and the power, and the glory forever. Amen.

5
Three Suggested
Remarriage Ceremonies

The sample ingredients from Chapter 4 should have given you some good ideas for planning your own wedding ceremony. Now let's look at three complete remarriage services to see how you can mix these elements together to form a ceremony with your own personal touch.

You could use one of these ceremonies just as it is printed here. Or, you might combine all three into one service that suits your personality as a couple a little better. Another approach is to use one of the services as a foundation, replacing specific elements with ingredients from Chapter 4 that seem to suit your style. Some of the ideas from these suggested remarriage ceremonies are sure to appeal to you and your fiancé as you search for just the right touch for your own wedding.

CEREMONY #1
TRADITIONAL VOWS
WITH A CONTEMORARY FLAIR

As you plan your remarriage ceremony, remember to balance innovative, contemporary elements with more traditional features from the past. This gives your ceremony a "just right" emotional appeal. The following service is a good example of this planning principle. The couple included their own personal touches but retained many traditional elements from the past, including the opening

words of the minister, Scripture passages on the meaning of mar-
riage, and the Lord's Prayer.

Prelude

"Praise to the Lord the Almighty"
"Jesu, Joy of Man's Desiring"

Vocal Music

"Though I Speak With the Tongues"

Processional

"Joyful, Joyful, We Adore Thee"

Opening Words of the Minister

We are assembled here in the presence of God and this company of friends to celebrate the joining of this man and this woman in holy matrimony. The covenant of marriage was established by God himself soon after his creation of the physical world. It was honored and blessed by the presence of Jesus at the wedding in Cana of Galilee. Marriage is also described in the New Testament as a symbol of the mystic union between Christ and his church. Marriage is fully commended in holy Scripture and is to be honored by all persons.

The uniting of husband and wife in heart, body, and spirit is intended by God for their mutual joy and satisfaction. Marriage should not be entered into lightly or unadvisedly, but reverently and in full accord with God's purpose. Into this holy relationship Andy and Juanita come now to be united. Let us pause and ask God's blessings upon this union.

Prayer of the Minister

Almight God our Father, giver of grace and joy, thank you for this special moment when your grace is revealed in such a wonderful way. Thank you for this couple, Andy and Juanita, as they ap-

51

proach this sacred moment in their lives. Thank you for bringing them together and nurturing their love for each other. And thank you for this company of friends who stand by them and support them as they pledge their devotion to each other through Christian marriage.

But above all, our Father, thank you for affirming and blessing marriage as life's most sacred human relationship. Grant that Andy and Juanita in their life together will find the supreme happiness and joy which you desire for all your children. Through Jesus Christ our Lord. Amen.

Exchange of Vows

MINISTER: Andy and Juanita, as you pledge your lives to each other in marriage, will you join hands and repeat after me:
> I, Andy (Juanita), take thee, Juanita (Andy),
> To be my wedded wife (husband),
> To have and to hold from this day forward;
> For better, for worse,
> For richer, for poorer,
> In sickness and in health;
> To love and to cherish 'til death do us part,
> According to God's holy ordinance.

Vocal Music

"Here at Thine Altar, Lord"

Exchange of Rings

MINISTER: From time immemorial the ring has been used to seal important covenants. Gold is a symbol of all that is pure, holy, and priceless. And the perfect circle of a ring signifies the eternity of God. Andy and Juanita, may your love for each other in the years ahead be as eternal and everlasting as these rings.

GROOM: (as he places the ring on the bride's finger): "Juanita, I offer you this ring as a symbol of my

BRIDE:

enduring love. I ask that you wear it to show others that you are touched by my love."

(*as she places the ring on the groom's finger*): "Andy, I also offer you this ring as a symbol of my everlasting love. I ask that you wear it to show others that you are touched by my love."

Remarks on Marriage by the Minister

Andy and Juanita, now that you have pledged yourselves to each other as husband and wife, I invite you to listen to the Bible's description of true love:

Love is patient and kind; it is not jealous or conceited or proud; love is not ill-mannered or selfish or irritable; love does not keep a record of wrongs; love is not happy with evil, but is happy with the truth. Love never gives up; and its faith, hope, and patience never fail (1 Cor. 13:4-7, TEV).

I charge you to cultivate this kind of love through all the days of your life together. God can help you practice this kind of love if you will call upon him for strength and guidance. Now let us pray together to ask God's blessings on your union.

Prayer by the Minister and Congregation

Eternal God our Father, look with favor upon these your servants, Andy and Juanita, who have pledged their love to each other here today. Grant that they may live together with peace, joy, and love, cultivating and renewing these vows day by day. And grant also that all married persons who have witnessed their vows may find their lives strengthened and their commitments reaffirmed. Now hear us as we pray together the Model Prayer our Lord taught us to pray, saying:

Our Father, who art in heaven, hallowed be thy name. Thy kingdom come, thy will be done, on earth as it is in heaven. Give us this day our daily bread. And forgive us our debts as we forgive our debtors. And lead us not into temptation, but deliver us from evil. For thine is the kingdom, and the power, and the glory forever. Amen.

53

Declaration of Marriage by the Minister

Andy and Juanita, since yo.. ..ve consented together in holy matrimony before God and this company of friends, and have exchanged vows and rings, pledging your lives to each other, I now pronounce that you are husband and wife, in accordance with God's holy ordinance. Whom therefore God has joined together, let no one put asunder.

Recessional

"Hymn to Joy"

CEREMONY #2
A SIMPLE SERVICE
FOR AN AT-HOME OR OUTDOOR WEDDING

Many couples getting married again prefer a simple no-frills approach, like the following ceremony. But notice that the couple did write their own vows and repeat them to each other at the appropriate place in the service. This one little personal touch made the ceremony uniquely their own. This service is especially suited for a simple at-home or outdoor wedding.

Opening Words of the Minister

We are gathered here today in the sight of God and in the presence of this company to join together Danny Knox and Kathryn Maxwell in holy matrimony. May our heavenly Father look upon this blessed event with his smile of approval. May the Lord Jesus Christ be present and add his blessing. May the Holy Spirit attend and seal these vows in love. For marriage is a divine ordinance given to promote social order and to ensure human happiness—and so it must remain until the end of time.

When God created man, he saw that it was not good for him to live alone. So he prepared a helpmate and companion to live with man and share his life. He took not the woman from man's head, lest she should rule over him, nor from his feet, lest he should trample upon her—but from his side, that she should be his equal, and from close to his heart, that he should love, cherish, and honor her.

Danny and Kathryn, let me remind you that marriage is one of the most important steps you will take in life. It should not be entered into lightly or unadvisedly but reverently, discreetly, and in the fear of God. Let us pause now to ask God's blessing upon your union.

Prayer of the Minister

O Lord our God, author of love and joy, thank you for this important moment of commitment in the lives of Danny and Kathryn. May their love for each other grow stronger with the passing years. Give them love and grace enough to forgive each other during those turbulent times in their relationship. Grant them also the gift of celebration so they can enjoy the many happy times they will share together as husband and wife. And most of all, our loving Father, keep their attention focused on you—the source and perfecter of every good gift of love. Through Jesus Christ our Lord. Amen.

Exchange of Vows

MINISTER: Danny and Kathryn, to symbolize your union, will you now join hands and repeat your wedding vows to each other.

GROOM: Kathryn, in this moment I celebrate the love we have shared since the day we met, and I look forward to the continuing growth of our love and respect in the days ahead. Today I choose you to be my wife, my friend, and the mother of our children. I promise to remain true to you through all the circumstances of life—in plenty and in want, in sickness and in health, in failure and in success. I will cherish and respect you, comfort and support you, so long as we both shall live.

BRIDE: Danny, in this moment I also celebrate the love we have shared since the day we met. And I, too, look forward to the growth and mutual cultivation of our love in the days ahead. Today I choose you to be my husband, my friend, and the father of our children. I promise to remain true to you through all the circumstances of life—in plenty and in want, in sickness and in health, in failure and in success. I will cherish

55

and respect you, comfort and support you, so long as we both shall live.

Exchange of Rings

MINISTER: Danny and Kathryn, you will now seal your vows through the act of giving and receiving the rings. The perfect circle of a ring symbolizes eternity. Gold is the symbol of all that is pure and holy. Our prayer is that your love for each other will be as priceless and precious as these rings. In the years to come they will remind you of this happy occasion. May you always be as happy with each other as you are in this sacred hour. Danny (*handing ring to the groom*), do you give this ring to Kathryn as a token of your love for her?

GROOM: I do.

MINISTER: Then place the ring on her finger and repeat after me.
I, Danny take thee, Kathryn,
To be my wedded wife;
To have and to hold from this day forward;
For better, for worse; for richer, for poorer;
In sickness and in health;
To love and to cherish 'til death do us part,
According to God's holy ordinance—
And thereto I pledge thee my love.

MINISTER: Kathryn (*handing ring to the bride*), do you give this ring to Danny as a token of your love for him?

BRIDE: I do.

MINISTER: Then place the ring on his finger and repeat after me.
I, Kathryn, take thee, Danny,
To be my wedded husband;
To have and to hold from this day forward;
For better, for worse; for richer, for poorer;
In sickness and in health;

To love and to cherish 'til death do us part,
According to God's holy ordinance—
And thereto I pledge thee my love.

Declaration of Marriage by the Minister

Danny and Kathryn, in these moments I have heard you pledge your faith and love to each other. Your friends and family members gathered here have witnessed the sealing of your marital vows as you have given and received the rings. Now, acting in the authority vested in me as a minister of the gospel, it is my joy and personal privilege to pronounce you husband and wife. Whom God has joined together, let not man put asunder.

CEREMONY #3
A CEREMONY OF
PARTICIPATION AND CELEBRATION

The following ceremony proves that a remarriage service doesn't have to be plain and ultra-simple. This couple wanted their family and friends to play a more active role in their wedding, so they included such features as responsive readings and hymn singing by the guests. In keeping with the theme of group interaction and participation, the bride and groom repeated their vows to each other in responsive fashion. A remarriage service of this type, of course, requires a wedding bulletin, with all responsive features printed in full for use by the guests.

Prelude

"Invocation"
"Ode to Joy"

Vocal Music

"Our Wedding Prayer"

Processional

"Processional on Westminster Abbey"

Opening Words of the Minister

In this sacred moment let all of us remember that God created human beings for togetherness. And Johnny and Debbie demonstrate the highest form of human togetherness as they express their desire to be united in the bonds of marriage. Please join me in reading responsively from their wedding bulletin to pledge your support to them as they take this important step in their lives.

Responsive Reading by Wedding Guests

MINISTER: Johnny and Debbie covet our prayers and support as they begin the pilgrimage of marriage together.

CONGREGATION: We promise to uphold them in our thoughts and prayers as they work at building a deep and everlasting love.

MINISTER: We must remind ourselves that genuine love is not easily achieved. Johnny and Debbie will need determination and patience to renew their vows year after year. Genuine love is not static; it must be constantly renewed.

CONGREGATION: We promise to support them in every appropriate way as they work at this task in their marriage.

MINISTER: We also realize that genuine love is fulfilled only as it reaches out to others. We ask that the unique love which Johnny and Debbie feel for each other might reach out beyond themselves to their family, their friends, and the larger world in which they live.

CONGREGATION: We promise to return this love as it flows out to us. And, we, in turn, will pass this love on to the larger universe in which we dwell. This is God's purpose in giving us the gift of love —that it might expand and grow to bless the lives of others.

Preparation for Exchange of Vows

MINISTER: Johnny and Debbie, you have heard this expression of support from your family and friends. Are you now prepared to seal your sacred union as husband and wife?

BRIDE AND GROOM: We are.

MINISTER: Then join hands and express your marriage vows to each other.

Exchange of Vows

GROOM: Debbie, I want to state it clearly so all the people here will understand: I love you and I want you to become my wife.

BRIDE: I gladly accept the privilege of becoming your wife. I also declare openly and honestly that I love you and I want you to become my husband.

GROOM: I promise to put you first in my life. I will always try to remember that our love for each other is our most important possession.

BRIDE: I also pledge to hold you first in my heart. I promise to work at building a strong, secure relationship that will stand the test of time and the ups and downs of life.

GROOM: I will be faithful to you always.

BRIDE: And I will be faithful to you.

UNISON: Whatever the future holds, we will face it together. We make these promises gladly in a spirit of joyful love.

Congregational Hymn

"Sweet, Sweet Spirit"

Exchange of Rings

MINISTER: The perfect circle of a ring symbolizes eternity, while gold is a symbol of all that is pure and holy. As you give these rings to each other, our

	prayer is that your love for each other will be as eternal and everlasting as these beautiful rings.
GROOM:	Debbie (*as he places the ring on her finger*), with this ring I symbolize our union as husband and wife—for today, tomorrow, and all the years to come. Please wear it as a reminder of our deep and abiding love.
BRIDE:	Johnny (*as she places the ring on his finger*), I also give you this ring as a symbol of our union as husband and wife—for today, tomorrow, and all the years to come. Please wear it as a reminder of our deep and abiding love.

Affirmation of Congregation

MINISTER:	All of you who have witnessed these vows (*turning to the congregation*), will you do everything in your power to support and uphold Johnny and Debbie in their marriage? Then say, "We will."
CONGREGATION:	We will.

Declaration of Marriage and Charge by the Minister

Johnny and Debbie, since you have made your marriage vows with each other and before all of us assembled here, I now pronounce that you are husband and wife, in accordance with God's holy purpose. Let me remind you to be merciful, kind, and forgiving toward each other. Accept life as a good gift from God and your marriage as an opportunity for highest fulfillment. Forgive each other as freely as God has forgiven you. And above all, be truly loving, growing in the knowledge and grace of the Lord Jesus Christ. Now you may light the unity candle to symbolize your union as husband and wife.

Lighting of the Unity Candle

MINISTER:	(*as bride and groom light the central candle with their individual candles*): The Bible declares that the man shall leave his home and

the woman shall leave her family and they shall become as one in a new relationship. In this mystic union they share a togetherness that gives them strength for all the circumstances of our earthly pilgrimage.

CONGREGATION: (*in unison*): As it was in the beginning, it is now until the end.

Concluding Prayer of the Minister

Eternal God our Father, go now with Johnny and Debbie on their journey into marriage. Impress the memories of this day upon their minds so they can draw strength and inspiration from this occasion in the days ahead. Fill them with such love and joy that they may build a loving, accepting, and forgiving home, in accordance with your will.

Now the Lord bless you and keep you; the Lord make his face to shine upon you, and be gracious unto you; the Lord lift up his countenance upon you and give you peace, both now and forevermore. Through Jesus Christ our Lord.

Presentation of the Couple by the Minister

It is my privilege to present to you Mr. and Mrs. Johnny Morgan.

Recessional

"Hymn to Joy"

6
Merging Two Households Into One

One of the first big jobs you will face after the wedding is merging two separate households into one. Actually, in most remarriages, this task begins as soon as the couple decide they are meant for each other. Every businessman knows that a merger of two companies takes a long time. You should also take the long view with your marriage merger. Don't expect it to happen overnight, and be prepared for some major adjustments.

Other remarried couples who have made this transition successfully indicate there are at least three big actions which the merger process demands. You and your spouse should: (1) recognize the power of possessions, (2) clear the air on the question of ownership, and (3) try to create a new living environment. Let's look at each of these actions in detail.

Recognize the Power of Possessions

The things they own tend to mean a great deal to people who have been married before. If you'll stop and think a minute, you'll understand why this is true.

Jack, for example, is "possession poor," but that's precisely why they mean so much to him. He and his wife were divorced after fifteen years of marriage. She was awarded the house and most of their furniture, since she gained custody of the children. Jack did manage to salvage a motorboat, his workshop equipment, and several odd pieces of furniture that were wedding gifts from his parents.

Most of the wounds from Jack's divorce have healed, but he still has the feeling that he was "ripped off" by the whole process. What would happen if Jack's new wife should suggest that he sell most of these items because they won't have room for them now that they're married? Jack would probably come out fighting like a cornered wildcat! His possessions from the past are more than things to him; they symbolize his manhood, his wounded pride, and his triumphant will to survive. It would be like cutting off a part of himself if he had to get rid of any of these.

Penny is another good example of this peculiar attitude toward possessions among those who have been divorced. Her husband abandoned the family and left her with the responsibility of rearing three children. At times she worked two jobs to make payments on the house and keep her children fed and clothed. It wasn't easy, but she managed on her own without receiving alimony and child-support payments. The house became hers when the divorce was finalized.

Years later, after Ben came into her life, Penny began to think about remarriage. But she was shocked when Ben suggested they sell her house to raise the down payment for a new home. That house was *hers*. She had worked hard to pay for it and keep her family together under its roof. It held years of memories for her and the children.

Penny's house was also something of a security blanket. She could always come back to it if her remarriage didn't work out. Could she really afford to take such a big risk with Ben? Look what happened before when she placed total trust in a spouse. To sell her house was a proposition that Penny would have to think about for a long time.

People who have been widowed also labor under the power of possessions from the past. Every item in Neal's house, for example, brought back pleasant memories of his marriage to Beth. From the china in the dining room to the wicker chair in the den, each object was special because she had either bought it, used it, or received it as a gift from him.

Now that Neal is dating again and actually thinking about remarriage, these possessions have lost some of their luster. But it would still take a very secure woman to agree to live in the "house of Beth." Neal must learn to loosen his hold on these possessions even more if he expects to build a successful relationship with another mate through remarriage—at least, in his house.

Notice the common theme that runs through these three examples. Their respective possessions are important to Jack, Penny, and Neal because of what these items symbolize, or represent, to them. You and your mate are wise, indeed, if you approach the whole business of possessions from the past with this principle clearly in mind.

When deciding how to sell, give away, or otherwise dispose of possessions in order to merge two households into one, try to use a light, sensitive touch. There's probably some good reason why your mate insists on keeping that ugly green sofa that looks absolutely horrible with the rest of your furniture. And the reason is probably tied up in the hidden meaning which the sofa holds for your spouse.

If you don't have room for all the furniture and other items which both of you insist on keeping, try to place the surplus items "on loan" in the homes of relatives or friends. Or, you might consider storing them for a while. After they are placed out of sight, they might begin to lose some of the hidden meaning which you or your mate have attached to them across the years. When this fades, you can dispose of them a lot easier.

But what about a house that one of you is reluctant to sell? Try not to make a big issue out of it. One mate really doesn't have the right to pressure the other to sell a piece of property against his or her will. This decision, too, might work out a little smoother after the two of you have lived together as husband and wife for a while.

In many remarriages where both mates own houses, both may elect to continue as individual owners of their respective pieces of property. One simply rents his or her house and moves in with the other. Income from the rental property is applied toward their joint household expenses. This seems to be a fair arrangement for everyone concerned.

One good thing to remember is that possessions become more important to all of us as we grow older. Increasingly, we find comfort and security in familiar objects from the past. It takes a little longer

64

for us to give up the old and familiar and to replace them with something new and strange.

You and your mate are older now than when you first married years ago. It's only natural that you should feel very strongly about some of your treasured possessions. Try to stay in touch with each other's feelings on this matter, particularly during the first few months of your marriage. This can help you keep possessions in their proper place in your life together as husband and wife.

Clear the Air on the Ownership Question

It's precisely because possessions are such an important factor in most second marriages that you and your mate need to take a practical, rational attitude toward them. Begin with a clear understanding of who owns what going into the marriage. Each of you should list the property and possessions you own as individuals. Then come to some agreement on the ownership terms you will follow in your marriage.

Many people going into a second marriage feel they really got burned on the property settlement agreement after their first marriage came apart. They're not as anxious to put all their possessions into joint ownership like they did the first time around. But here's one approach which seems to work well for many couples: Each retains individual title to the things they own going into the second marriage. But the items they buy to service their household after they get married are considered their joint property, with each holding equal shares.

Hazel and Bryan are a good example of how this arrangement works. When they married, Hazel owned a portfolio of stocks and bonds, awarded to her as a part of the property settlement in her divorce several years before. Bryan owned a farm which he had inherited from his father since his divorce from his first wife. The couple agreed that each would retain title to these properties and use them to pay the college expenses of their respective children when they reached that age in several years.

Meanwhile, Hazel and Bryan also bought a house together as husband and wife to get their remarriage off on the right foot. This piece of property they purchased under a joint-ownership agreement, with each sharing equally in their right to the property.

A remarriage involving a person who has lost his or her spouse through death requires some extra levelheaded thinking about the matter of property ownership. A person in this situation is more likely to own substantial assets because of insurance settlements and inheritance of the previous mate's share of all their property.

Mona, for example, didn't date any men for several years after the death of her husband. She feared they were all "bounty hunters" who were trying to get their hands on a piece of the $100,000 life insurance settlement which she had stashed away in the bank. And, being a realistic woman, she realized her adult children might object to her remarriage unless they were assured of getting their share of their father's estate some day.

After taking her time and finding the right man, Mona eventually did remarry. But she and her husband agreed that a large portion of her estate should be placed in a trust fund for her children's eventual inheritance. With his aid and encouragement, Mona worked out all the arrangements and had them recorded legally as a part of her will even before her wedding day. This cleared the air on the ownership question and helped Mona's marriage get started on a positive note.

While we're on the subject of wills, remember to make any needed changes in yours before or soon after your remarriage. If you have never had a will, now's a good time to have one drawn up. This is true for wives as well as husbands. Each of you might want a separate will for the benefit of your respective children as well as a joint will with instructions for disposition of the property that you own together.

There's a lot more to a second marriage than the things that both of you own, either individually or together. But sometimes, "things" can prevent the development of a deep relationship unless you deal with them properly from the very beginning. This time around you ought to be mature adults who can discuss such matters openly and honestly. Do yourselves a favor and clear the air on the ownership question well before your wedding day rolls around.

Create a New Living Environment

Another problem for most couples in second marriages is the actual space in which their families will live. Your chances of success are greater if you realize the need to create a new living environment for the unique family that emerges when all of you are blended into one.

Most "blended families" realize that the ideal arrangement would be a brand new living space. If you and your mate and the children from your previous marriages move into a new house soon after you're married, all of you will be on level ground, so to speak. None of you will feel like a stranger or an intruder on the other's familiar turf. This forces all of you to adjust to a totally new living arrangement. And the very act of coping together can draw all of you closer together as a family.

But a new house is out of the question in most remarriage situations. Most couples just can't afford the higher payments that a different or larger place would demand. So the trick is getting the whole family together into one of your existing places with a minimum of disruption. It helps if you realize from the very beginning that this is a tall order. It will tax every ounce of your patience and ingenuity.

To realize just how tough it is, let's think about a typical situation where two families are brought together under the same roof. This case involves Sam and Judy and their assorted offspring.

Sam, a father of three, had custody of his teenage son. They lived together in a small apartment until Sam and Judy decided to get married. The couple agreed that Sam and son would move into the house with Judy and her two children, a daughter, age 10, and a son, age 12. They really didn't think of the merger of the two families as a big deal, requiring a lot of adjustment, since only five people were involved. Surely all of them could fit comfortably into a three-bedroom house.

Sam's son moved into the bedroom with Judy's son. To accommodate the two, they bought a set of bunk beds. The boys seemed to hit it off fine for the first few weeks. But then each began to complain to his respective parent.

Sam's son was finding the small bedroom cramped and confining, especially since he had enjoyed a room of his own at Sam's apartment. Judy's son was even more vocal in his complaints. He resented Sam's son for barging into his territory and taking up most of the space with his stereo and huge record collection. This strange new arrangement, he whimpered, was making him feel like a stranger in his own house.

After their sons broke the ice with their complaints, Sam and Judy felt freed up enough to confront each other about their respective problems with the living arrangements. Sam ventilated his frustrations about not feeling at ease in the house because of Judy's determination to do things in her old familiar way. For example, she poured cold water on Sam's suggestion about starting a vegetable garden in the backyard. Her refusal to negotiate the issue left Sam feeling like a tenant in a boarding house. He could live there, but he had no say in how the place was run.

Judy also got in her share of complaints. She was particularly disturbed at how Sam's two daughters seemed to take over the place when they came for their weekend visits about once per month. They made snide remarks about Judy's daughter, refused to include her in their games, and wouldn't lift a finger to help with chores while they were there. By the end of one of these weekends, July felt fatigued and frustrated. And Sam, according to her, contributed to the problem. He seemed to think that the girls' visits were to be weekends of fun and games. Chores were for the rest of the family.

As far-fetched as this case may sound, it's actually a good representation of some of the problems you can expect when one mate moves into the residence of the other. Especially is this true when both of you have children who will live with you in the house.

You and your offspring will be giving up the familiar space you have grown accustomed to. And the family you are moving in with will also find its living pattern drastically changed. The danger is that you and your children will feel powerless and out of place in someone else's house, while they will feel inconvenienced and "put upon" by these "guests" who have moved in for good.

Here are some things you can do to head off these feelings and make the merger of two households a more positive experience for everyone concerned.

1. Try to look ahead and anticipate some of the major disruptions that both families might experience. Talk about these as husband and wife and review them openly and honestly with your children. Your ability to confront these practical problems on the

68

front end will automatically take some of the emotional trauma out of the household merger.

2. If possible, make some changes in the way the household space is being used to prepare the way for the merger. For example, if one of your children will be sharing a bedroom with one of your mate's children, have your spouse's child swap bedrooms a month or so before you and your offspring move in. This little bit of strategy will minimize that child's sense of disruption at having a stranger move in to occupy his familiar territory. The bedroom will be somewhat new to both of them from the very beginning.

Another change might involve the dining room. Perhaps your mate and his or her children have always eaten at the small breakfast table in the kitchen. When you and your children move in, agree that the merged family will eat at the large table in the dining room. This gives your blended family a brand new routine that all of you can share in equally from the very start of your life together.

3. Think about making some physical changes in the space that all of you will be occupying. Just before or soon after the other family moves in is an ideal time for a major remodeling project, if your finances will allow it. Merged families are larger families, so additional space may be needed in the form of an extra bedroom, a larger den, an additional bath, etc. This gives the blended family a new living arrangement that every member can grow accustomed to at the same time.

4. Try to avoid the temptation to settle all your children's squabbles over "territorial rights." Do let them know that you're concerned about the problem. But they, after all, will have to learn to work the problem out between them if physical changes are impossible. Sometimes this strong message from the parents will give children the encouragement they need to search for a solution that each of them can live with.

5. Finally, remember that merging two households into one is a long-term process rather than a one-time event. This attitude should help you as your two respective families work at the task of becoming one. You'll know you're making progress when all of you stop thinking in terms of *they* and *them* and begin using words like *we* and *our*. This is a cause for celebration in the life of any blended family.

While you're working at the task of becoming a harmonious family unit, you'll probably be facing some other key adjustments as well. Move on to the next chapter for a thorough discussion of three of these that seem to be a part of most remarriage relationships.

7
Coping With Major Remarriage Adjustments

If your former marriage taught you anything, it should have dispelled the "living happily ever after" myth. Two people don't just stumble into a relationship as intimate as marriage and find instant happiness and success. They have to work at building a good relationship. This is a task that's never finished. You have to keep on working at it as long as you live together as husband and wife.

If this is true for first-time marriages, how much more does the principle apply to remarriage relationships. While you may be more levelheaded and mature the second time around, remember that you also face some unique adjustments that grow out of your status as formerly married persons. You and your mate will be better equipped to cope with these adjustments if you enter your marriage with a realistic attitude toward these tensions and their demands.

The three big pressure points in most remarriages are money, ex-mates, and stepchildren. Let's take a careful look at each of these for some insights on what to expect.

Money

Money doesn't seem like such a big deal to many couples when they consider remarriage. After all, they love each other, they remind themselves, and this should make it easy to handle any problems that might come along.

Don't be misled by this shallow way of thinking. Money matters can be a source of difficulty in a remarriage. The best thing you and your fiancé can do is to discuss your financial situation openly and honestly before your wedding day. You need to agree on how you will handle certain delicate money situations after your two separate families are merged into one.

Bob and Alice are a good example of how this procedure should work. They realized money could become a real problem in their relationship unless they agreed on some important ground rules. Both had children from their former marriages. Bob was making child-support payments to his ex-wife, who had custody of their two children. And Alice was receiving payments from her ex-husband to help with the expense of providing home for their three daughters.

This couple agreed that both would continue to maintain separate checking accounts after their marriage. Bob would write child-support checks to his ex-wife from his account, while Alice would deposit her child-support payments in her separate account. She would draw from this account to pay many of the expenses involved in providing for her girls, including food, clothing, shelter, and school expenses.

Bob and Alice agreed they would share all additional household expenses on a fair and equitable basis, based on the income which each received from his respective job. Since Bob earned a higher salary, his share of their household expenses—after meeting his obligations to his own children—would be proportionately higher than Alice's share.

After testing this financial arrangement in their marriage, Bob and Alice found that it seemed to work well for them. It helped them meet the obligations that grew out of their previous marriages while contributing their fair share to their current family situation at the same time. They avoided a potential problem over money and how it would be divided by reaching some basic agreements in advance.

Contrast Bob and Alice's careful planning with the lack of foresight which George and Jennifer displayed. Each of them also had children from previous marriages. Jennifer realized that George had some responsibility for supporting his children, but somehow they never got around to talking about specifics.

Unknown to George, Jennifer thought of her approaching marriage as a chance to escape the nine-to-five ratrace that she had been living since her divorce. She had gone to work to support herself and the children, but she had hated every minute of it. After marrying George, she told herself, she could quit her job and go back to being a fulltime wife and mother again.

Imagine this couple's shock after their marriage when the truth began to emerge. Jennifer did quit her job, expecting George to carry the full load of supporting her and the children. This forced him to confess that he couldn't do it on his own, since he was paying several hundred dollars a month in alimony and child support on behalf of his ex-wife and children.

Suddenly, a remarriage that had been launched with great expectations was caught up in a perilous financial storm. The tragedy is that this could have been avoided if George and Jennifer had leveled with each other about their financial limitations and expectations *before* the wedding day.

These two examples show very clearly that remarried couples with children are prime prospects for financial pressures. And even if you and your mate have a good idea of the required financial commitments going into a marriage, this is no guarantee that the situation will remain orderly and predictable.

Remarriage of one's former spouse often brings out the worst in a person. For example, a man may quit sending child-support payments as soon as his ex-wife remarries. Or, an ex-wife may demand extra money from her former husband in addition to regular child support, as soon as she learns he has taken a new wife. While you might recognize these as games of revenge and psychological manipulation, how would you react if these were pulled on you and your new mate?

Could you make it financially as a family if that monthly child-support check were suddenly cut off? Going back to court to force the ex-husband to pay could take several months and be expensive. How would you handle an ex-wife's plea for extra money to spend on your children? In remarriages where children from previous relationships are involved, you are wise, indeed, if you consider all these possibilities and talk about them seriously. Don't be paralyzed by neurotic fear about all the things that could happen. On the other hand, try to be prepared for any possibility. Other remarried couples before you have found this to be a wise and resourceful course of action.

Another reality about money management that catches many remarried couples by surprise are the two separate, independent systems they have developed during their lives as formerly married persons. Each has grown accustomed to spending his money as he pleases without answering to anyone else. After marriage, they must learn to work together as a couple again in managing their financial resources.

Even if a husband and wife decide to keep their own separate checking accounts and manage some of their finances as individuals, this should be a decision which both of them make together. In a marriage each deserves to be fully informed about the other's finances, even though the management of those funds may be the sole responsibility of one person.

This unwritten rule about keeping the other fully informed on financial matters is one of the pillars of a secure marriage. One of the quickest ways for a husband or wife to undermine this foundation is to try to hide part of his income or assets from the other.

Harry let this happen in his remarriage to Irene. A middle-aged businessman, he never told her about the substantial income which he received from his investment in a large shopping center complex. Irene discovered it when an article about the mall—complete with Harry's name as one of the investors—appeared in the local paper.

After a confrontation with Irene, he admitted he had kept the investment from her because of a hidden fear. Harry had lost practically everything he owned in his divorce from his first wife, and he was afraid it might happen again unless he kept some of his property "in reserve," as he tactfully put it.

This explanation came across to Irene as nothing more than lack of trust. It made her wonder what other secrets Harry had hidden away. Only after they talked the issue out thoroughly with the aid of a professional counselor was the element of mutual trust restored to their marriage.

The high cost of housing is another surprise to remarried couples, unless they take their time in choosing an adequate, affordable place

74

to live. Your first thought may be that you will actually save money when your two families are merged into one, since this eliminates the double expense of maintaining two households. But this bonanza probably won't materialize at all if you have to buy a new or larger house for your merged family. The soaring inflation and higher interest rates of recent years have combined to push the monthly payments on newer houses right through the ceiling.

Try to remember that the decision you make about housing will be with you for a long time in the form of regular monthly payments. Precisely because it's such a key financial decision, you should take your time in deciding what housing arrangement fits your budget as well as the needs of your merged family.

Your first step may be to get both families together into one of the apartments or houses where one of you has been living. Then, as you evaluate your space requirements from the practical realities of living together, you can start looking around for new housing that suits your needs as well as your budget.

While you're thinking about the practical side of money management, consider the peace of mind which a good life insurance program can bring to a remarriage situation. If both you and your mate have children, for example, you can take some of the pressure off the other regarding the uncertainties of the future by providing for your children financially in the event of your death. This goes for women as well as men.

If you're a mother who has custody of your children in a remarriage, you really can't afford to depend on their father to step in and assume custody if you should die. Even if he could swing it financially, this might not be the best for the children. And would it be fair to your new husband to expect him to take on that responsibility all alone, expecially if he has children of his own to support?

When you look at the situation like this, you realize that adequate life insurance for you, their mother, makes a lot of sense. Early in your remarriage talk this out thoroughly with your mate and decide on a plan that provides adequate protection for everyone in your blended family.

These aren't the only money issues you'll face in your marriage. But these should be enough to give you a good idea of the unique circumstances that surround the blending of two families into one. If you can learn to confront financial pressures head-on in a practical, realistic approach, you are well on your way toward the goal of a happy, fulfilling marriage.

Ex-Mates

Another adjustment that you can expect in a second marriage grows out of the very nature of remarriage itself. You and your spouse are taking on new mates, but you can't get around the fact that you have been married before. These "ghosts from the past" have a strange way of coming back to haunt you, even if your second marriage is relatively happy and fulfilling from the very first.

It might help if you can admit as you start out together that remarriage always involves a double adjustment—breaking free of the past relationship as well as committing yourself to the new "number one person" in your life. One of these alone would be tough enough, but you and your mate will have to handle both of these tasks at the same time. Patience and mutual understanding are essential as you work your way through this period of adjustment.

Most people who remarry feel they have put the old relationship behind them. But the facts don't bear this out. The act of remarriage itself often brings back a lot of strong feelings that haven't been fully resolved. Guilt is one of the strongest of these emotions.

Mel is a perfect example of the guilt-ridden spouse. After nine years of marriage, he asked for a divorce because of his attraction to another woman. In the settlement agreement, he made sure his former wife and the children were well cared for. Even after his remarriage to Anita he stayed in constant contact with his ex-wife to make sure she and the children were all right. Without consulting Anita, he gave them extra money on several occasions to buy expensive clothes, toys, and other luxuries. This angered Anita, since she felt that she and her children were coming in "second" on Mel's priority list.

The problem with excessive guilt like this is that it can be so easily misinterpreted by the current mate. In addition to her frustration over his actions, Anita was also bewildered. She wondered if Mel still loved his first wife and secretly yearned to go back to her. She and Mel must recognize his feelings for what they are and talk them out thoroughly before they can develop a deep relationship as husband and wife.

Lingering resentment toward a former mate is another emotion that can cause problems in a remarriage. Lisa, for example, was deeply hurt by her unfortunate experience with an immature husband the first time around. His wild and impulsive spending on boats, hunting gear, and other expensive hobbies eventually drove them into bankruptcy and divorce.

Lisa wound up so resentful of her ex-husband and these expensive "men's toys" that she pitched a fit one day when Hank, her second husband, brought an inexpensive fishing rod that he had bought on sale. She refused to compromise on the issue and insisted that he take it back immediately. Hank gave in that time, but he made a mental note of their need to discuss the problem. Hank has the right to be judged on his own merits and not victimized by Lisa's lingering resentment toward her former mate.

Another negative emotion from the past that can cause problems in a remarriage is fear. Joe and Marilyn are a perfect example of this peculiar dynamic at work in a relationship. Several years before she met and married Joe, Marilyn lost her husband to a heart attack. She was attracted to Joe partly because he had also lost a spouse, but under different circumstances. After twenty-five years of what he thought was a happy marriage, Joe came home one day to find a farewell note from his wife. He never saw her again, and he finally filed for divorce on the grounds of abandonment.

On the surface, Joe and Marilyn appear to have a good marriage. But they are really clinging to each other out of fear more than anything else. Joe won't let his new wife out of his sight, and Marilyn badgers him constantly with reminders to take care of himself. They are afraid of losing each other, as they did with their first marriage partners. Their relationship is only skin deep, since they're hesitant to confront each other and explore their differences. The tragedy is that their "closeness" actually hinders the development of a deep and intimate marriage relationship.

Since negative emotions from the past are such a potent force in remarriage, they are where you should begin in trying to build a good relationship with your current mate. Here are some questions for both of you to ask yourselves and discuss together as you try to put the past behind you:

- What caused the most pain for each of you in your previous marriages? What coping mechanisms did you use in dealing with the pain? What progress have you made in dealing with the "fall-out" of a broken marriage?
- Can you think of your ex-mate now and reflect on the experiences you shared without being immobilized by guilt, resentment, or fear? What about positive experiences? Can you recall some of the good things you shared?
- Have you tried consciously to forgive your ex-mate for the pain and humiliation you suffered in your previous marriage?
- Have you tried consciously to forgive yourself for the hurt you brought to others in your former relationship?
- What are some of the valuable lessons you have learned about yourself and life in general as a result of your first marriage relationship and its dissolution?

If you and your mate will take the time to probe these questions early in your remarriage, it could save you a lot of agony later on. If they accomplish nothing else, the questions should at least establish a climate of openness and honesty in your relationship. And this can make a big difference in your ability to confront problems and search for sound solutions.

Strange as it may seem, a previous mate's good points can also put pressure on a remarriage. When you reach the point where you can recall your former spouse's assets as well as his liabilities, you are probably making real progress in your adjustment to a second marriage. At least, this indicates that you aren't overreacting to the negatives of the past in your current relationship. But try to remember that this may not come across in exactly that way to your current mate. He or she may be threatened by this acknowledgment of your ex-spouse's skills and abilities.

Byron and Susan discovered this truth in their relationship. During the first year or so of their remarriage, Byron never mentioned his former wife except in derogatory terms. Then he suddenly began to pay her little compliments about the way she dressed, cooked, played tennis, etc. This caught Susan by surprise, and she demanded an explanation.

"Oh, I didn't realize I was doing that," Byron replied. "I guess I just finally admitted to myself that she did have some pretty good points. But don't worry, Susan; I'm not comparing you to her. I like this marriage just the way it is."

Just like Susan, most husbands and wives in remarriage situations are quick to pick up on any remark about a previous mate's skills, no matter how innocent the reference may be. A wife has been known to knock herself out to become a better cook than her husband's "ex," for example, because she misread his remark about a certain dish she used to fix. Or, a husband who is strictly all thumbs may try to become a first-class handyman because his wife's first husband, according to her, "was always fixing things around the house."

You and your mate can save yourselves a lot of hassle if you will learn to talk about these things before rushing into a fit of compulsive behavior, trying to prove your superiority. Learn to confront each other openly and honestly until you discover the real meaning behind the remark. Make sure you spend your creative energies attacking the *real* problem—not what seems to be the issue from your limited perspective.

Maybe you have heard these words about relationships from an old English folk song. They have a real message for remarried couples:

It is good to be merry and wise,
It is good to be honest and true,
It is best to be off with the old love
Before you are on with the new.

During the first few months of your life together, old wounds and memories from the past may come crashing in on your relationship. But this should become less and less of a problem as you talk things out and move through this period of adjustment. Mutual understanding is essential as you go through the process of casting off the old and putting on the new. In time, your relationship should blossom into the new adventure in mutual discovery that every remarried couple has the right to expect.

Stepchildren

Perhaps the greatest adjustment you will face if either you or your mate have children will be establishing a good relationship with your stepchildren. In most studies of remarriages conducted by social researchers, this emerges as the number one issue. Even before you get married again, you and your mate-to-be should begin discussing your blended family, trying to look at the situation from the point of view of any children involved.

You can take hope in the fact that other remarried couples before you have weathered this experience successfully. And they have gained some valuable insights that can help you through this phase of remarriage adjustment.

Be realistic in your expectations. The first good piece of advice that other stepparents have to offer is to enter your marriage with a realistic attitude toward stepchildren and the challenge of taking on this new role. Don't psych yourself out with negative thoughts about how terrible the experience is going to be. On the other hand, don't tell yourself that it's going to be instant happiness and success on a calm, unruffled sea. The best approach is to be cautiously optimistic—expect the best but be prepared to handle the worst, if it should happen.

Your attitudes and expectations are crucial, because they can become a stumbling block that slows down the relationship-building process. Peggy is a perfect example of this problem. She naively assumed that her teen-age stepdaughter would welcome her with open arms as soon as she married her father. But Gloria was actually jealous and resentful when Peggy moved in and began rearranging the house to suit her style. Peggy was so shocked by this rude reception that she went into a pouting routine that made the problem even worse.

How much better prepared Peggy would have been to become a stepparent if if she had been realistic about some of the possible problems from the very start. She had to work through the shock of her dashed expectations before she could tackle the task of building a good relationship with Gloria.

People who set themselves up for the biggest shock of all in a remarriage are those who see themselves as "rescuers" of the step-children. For example, a woman with no children may look forward to her marriage to a man who has custody of his children from a previous marriage. These children need a loving mother, she reasons, and she can hardly wait to begin filling this void in their lives.

But if the children are the least bit cool or hesitant about accepting her as their "instant mother," she feels hurt and rejected. How could they be so ungrateful, she asks herself, when she has made such a sacrifice to rescue them from their motherless plight?

Just as you need to be cautious about your expectations of your stepchildren, don't expect your own children to form an instant attachment to their stepparent and the new circumstances surrounding your remarriage. Keep reminding yourself that your new life will represent a big change in their accustomed way of doing things. And adjusting to change, even for children, takes a certain amount of time. Cool, realistic, level-headed thinking like this can get you off on the right foot with your stepchildren and keep your expectations in line.

Consider the losses your children may be feeling. Another principle that can keep you on a steady course is to remember that you and your mate are entering remarriage from a totally different perspective than the children. Your remarriage represents another chance for happiness and fulfillment to the two of you. But it may be painful for the children because it symbolizes the losses which they are experiencing.

Most children whose parents have been divorced live under the constant delusion that their parents will get back together again. Even after you begin to date other people seriously, they may continue to nurture this secret dream. But your remarriage punctures this mythical balloon with a giant bang. Their sense of loss and the natural period of grief which goes along with it may come out in the form of negative feelings. The stepparent generally catches most of this fall-out, since he or she is the one who ended their hidden fantasy.

This fading of a dream is a common experience among the children of the remarried, no matter what their ages. But another loss which older children and teen-agers sometimes feel is the loss of a role.

Edward, for example, had become the "man of the house" for his mother since his parents' divorce. She relied on him to do yard and lawn work and even to help support the family through his part-time job. But all that changed when Edward's mother remarried. His stepfather took over the maintenance work around the house and let it be known that his salary was adequate to support the family. Suddenly, Edward felt like a discarded pair of worn-out shoes, useless and unwanted. No wonder he tended to be resentful. And his stepfather's lack of sensitivity didn't make it any easier.

In your remarriage, be particularly aware of the loss that an older stepchild may feel at your presence if this child has been carrying heavy responsibility in the family. A teen-age stepdaughter who has helped run the household may be particularly threatened if you come on like gangbusters and begin to reorganize all the routines she has established. A wise stepparent will be sensitive and aware in a situation like this and try to enlist the older child as an ally and helper in the adjustment process.

Another emotion which many children go through at the remarriage of their parents is resentment over being replaced as the number one person in their parents' lives. Single parents and their children often develop a very close relationship because they depend on each other so much for emotional support. It hurts when the parent remarries and the child realizes his mother or father doesn't need him as much as he did before. It's only natural that the child be a little jealous and resentful toward the stepparent who has taken over his favored position.

In cases like this, both the stepparent and the natural parent need to reassure their children that they don't love them any less because they are getting remarried. Help them to understand that they will always have a special place in your lives. Make sure your actions reinforce this verbal message. Above all, be patient and understanding as your children try to sort out these various changes that are taking place within the family.

Occasionally, a child may feel so let down and betrayed by the remarriage of his custodial parent that he insists on going to live with his other parent. This could be his way of coping with a sense of rejection and the feeling that he is losing his special place in your affections.

If this should happen to you, try to talk it out with the child and stall for time. He may change his mind after he lives under the remarriage situation and realizes that your love for him really hasn't changed. But make sure he understands that you won't let him break up your marriage. In extreme cases, it might be necessary for him to go to live with the other parent for a while. As a part of the agreement, assure him that the door is always open if he changes his mind and wants to come back home.

Give the relationship time to develop. It's precisely because of the unique adjustments that children face because of their parents' remarriage that you need to give your relationship time to grow and develop. One of the worst mistakes you can make is to expect your stepchildren to accept you immediately, displaying instant love and respect. Your relationship could begin on a cool note and grow progressively deeper over a period of several years.

To understand why this is true, try to think about the situation from the perspective of your stepchild. He may have a lot of conflicting feelings over the remarriage of his custodial parent. He probably feels just as uncomfortable about being a stepchild as you do about being a stepparent. He still loves his other natural parent, although he may see him or her only occasionally during visitation weekends. He probably wonders how he can remain loyal to his real father or mother and be open and accepting toward you as a stepparent at the same time.

It's very natural for a stepchild to hold a stepparent at arm's length for a while until he learns how to reconcile these internal conflicts. In time he will realize that it's possible to love the stepparent as well as the natural parent without being disloyal to either of you. You can help this process of learning and adjustment by taking a slow and easygoing approach. Let your relationship develop naturally rather than trying to force it to suit your timetable.

Some stepparents make the mistake of insisting that their stepchildren express affection toward them from the very beginning of their relationship. Remember that a hug or a kiss means very little if you have to ask for them. They will mean a great deal more to everyone concerned if they are given spontaneously after you and the stepchildren develop a secure and comfortable relationship.

The same goes for the question of an appropriate name which the children should use in referring to you. Recognize that they may feel uncomfortable calling you "Mom" or "Dad," since you are not their natural mother or father. Put them at ease about this from the very beginning by telling them they can call you by your first name if they prefer. As your relationship develops, they may coin their own personal name for you that symbolizes their growing love and affection.

Don't try too hard. Another good piece of advice that veteran stepparents offer to novices in the game is to relax a little about the task you're taking on. Many stepparents go into a blended family with a grim and determined attitude as if the whole world turned on their performance. You'll become your own worst enemy if you put this much pressure on yourself.

Andrea, for example, was so determined to make a happy home for Joe and his two daughters that she ignored their cutting remarks and let them get by with all kinds of atrocious behavior. She was afraid they might resent it if she as their stepmother tried to make them toe the line. They were old enough to help out around the house, but she was hesitant to insist that they pull their share of the load.

Things might have gotten totally out of hand if Andrea hadn't become angry one day when both girls demanded that she get their favorite outfits ready for a party that night. It was the last straw for Andrea, since she had been through a very busy and demanding day. She came down hard on the girls about their selfishness and lack of consideration and cooperation.

This little outburst seemed to break the ice between Andrea and the girls. They warmed up to her considerably when she dropped the "kid gloves" approach and showed them she cared enough about the family to insist that they do their part of the work. After this incident, Andrea also learned to quit trying so hard to be a "perfect stepmother" and to relate to the girls on the basis of her true feelings.

One of the problems with bending over backwards for the stepchildren is that you might lose the respect of your own children. They will notice quickly if you have one level of expectations for them and a second for the stepchildren. If you can't confront the stepchildren yourself because of the delicate nature of the situation, then you and your mate need to have a meeting of the minds. It's imperative that the two of you present a united front about the type of behavior required of *all* the children who live in the household.

Here's another subtle clue that may show you're trying a little too hard to make your blended family operate smoothly. It can happen if your children come to you with complaints about their step

84

parent. Do you listen carefully and agree to take up this problem with your mate? Or, do you listen like a good parent and then encourage them to talk it out with the stepparent on their own? In most cases, it's much better to let your children work out their problem with the stepparent face to face.

If you find yourself getting caught in the middle of these little spats, you're probably accepting more than your fair share of responsibility for family harmony and success. By your actions you and your mate can show your children that each of them has a responsibility to work out relationship problems in order to make the blended family a pleasant place to live.

The problem with being a grim and uptight stepparent is that you operate as if the success of the family depends totally on you. But a blended family is unique in that every member of the union must do his fair share of compromise and negotiation in order to make the relationship work. It will help if you keep reminding yourself, *there is no shortcut to instant happiness and success.*

Some experts believe it takes about five years for the members of a typical blended family to work out all the relationships to the point where they feel comfortable and secure with one another. If that's true, you only complicate the problem by adopting the stance of a "super stepparent" and trying to solve all the conflicts on your own.

Maintain ties with the children away from home. Another tension that many stepparents feel is tying to cultivate close ties with their children who visit them only occasionally, since they are in the custody of other parents. Trying to adjust to their periodic visits is tough on everyone in the family. But just think what it must be like to the child who drops in for these visitation weekends.

Little Eddie, for example, reached the point where he dreaded his periodic visits with his father. He always felt like a stranger in the house, since his stepmother's three children did very little to make him feel welcome. They went on with their games and other activities without including him. On most weekends he just moped around and watched television until his father took him back to his mother's home on Sunday afternoon.

If you're in a situation where a child from a previous marriage makes periodic visits to your home, you need to talk about this as a faimly and adopt a welcoming strategy. The children who live with you permanently should accept their share of this responsibility. Talk about ways the visiting child could be included in their activities.

Above all, you as a parent should make it a point to do something special with your child during his visits. This doesn't have to be a spectacular production, like horseback riding or a trip to the zoo. The main thing is that the two of you share some special experience that underlines your relationship as parent and child. Occasionally, you may need to get away from the house where you can concentrate on each other without the distractions of your mate and the stepchildren. Sharing special moments like these can assure your child of your continuing love and concern, although you don't see him as often as his other parent.

* * *

Money, ex-mates, and stepchildren—these are the three adjustments that will probably give you the most trouble in your remarriage relationship. If it gets to be more than you can handle on your own, don't hesitate to seek the services of a professional counselor.

Recognizing when you need an objective viewpoint is a sign of strength, not weakness. But don't wait until the situation gets beyond the point of no return. The best approach is to enter remarriage with a commitment to seek professional help at the first sign of trouble which the two of you can't resolve. Your first marriage should have taught you that it's not a crime to have problems in a relationship. The real tragedy is to do nothing while you and your mate drift farther and farther apart.

What remarried couples need as they face their life together is the ability to dream without being carried away by their euphoria—a positive attitude tempered with a strong dose of realism. If you can hold these two elements in tension in your relationship, you are well on the way toward building a happy and fulfilling marriage the second time around.

8
Typical Questions About Remarriage and Second Weddings

Some questions about remarriage and second weddings come up quite frequently. Maybe you'll find many of your questions answered in this quick-reference section.

When should I tell my children that I'm planning to remarry?

As a general rule, within a few days after you and your fiancé decide there's a wedding in your future. This will give them plenty of time to get used to the idea of your remarriage and bring their concerns to you so you can air them together. Your remarriage will bring about some major changes in their lives, and it makes sense to get the adjustment process started as soon as possible.

What about letting our children participate in the wedding? Is this considered appropriate?

Yes, by all means, if your children want to be involved. Some appropriate roles they could fill include flower girls, ring bearers, ushers, groomsmen, and attendants—maybe even a best man, in the case of an older teen-age son. But don't force your children to participate in the ceremony if they feel reluctant or uncomfortable about doing so.

My older teen-age son and I have discussed the possibility of him giving me away during my wedding. But some of my friends don't think this would be appropriate. What's your opinion?

One of the taboos about remarriage is that a woman should not be "given away" again after she has been through this ceremonial in her first wedding. Your son could simply serve as your escort and stand with you during the ceremony without going through the "who gives this woman ..." routine. This should be sufficient to make him feel involved in this significant moment in your life.

I realize a woman who has been married before is not supposed to wear a long white wedding dress. But this is the first marriage for my fiancé, and he wants me to look the part of a radiant, "storybook" bride. What should I do?

If this is such an important point to the groom, you may have to bend the rules a little and dress to suit his fantasy. No matter what the rule books say, the main thing is to make your wedding a unique expression of your hopes and dreams. Just be aware that you're going against tradition but you have a valid reason for doing so.

What about costs? Who pays for a second wedding?

In most remarriages, the bride and groom share equally in all expenses of the wedding. The one exception to this general rule is a wedding where a never-married woman becomes the wife of a previously married man. It's considered appropriate for the bride's parents to bear most of the expenses in this case.

I'm a second-time bride, but my parents still insist on paying for the wedding. What should I do?

Talk it over with your fiancé and see how he feels about it. If he has no objection, there's no reason why you can't accept their offer. But make sure you think it over thoroughly before saying yes. Many remarried couples have reported that the experience of planning and paying for their wedding brought them closer together and got them off on a sound footing as husband and wife.

The matter of a name change has me confused. Do I have to take my new husband's last name after my remarriage?

Different states have different laws on this matter, and they have tended to become more relaxed in recent years. Many professional women may enjoy some distinct advantage in using the previous name they have established and built across the years. Your children, of course, will continue to bear the last name of their biological father, no matter what your marital status or surname change. If the matter of a name change is important to you, talk it over with your fiancé and see how he feels about it. The two of you might seek legal counsel together to see what state laws apply if you decide to keep your name from a previous marriage.

The minister at my church refuses to officiate at my wedding, since I have been divorced. I would like to get married in a church ceremony. What can I do?

Check with your minister about scheduling the wedding at the church and enlisting another minister to perform the service. If this is impossible, seek another church with a more open policy where the service could be held. Florists in the community might have some leads on houses of worship where your wedding would be welcomed.

I'm remarrying the same person to whom I was married for eight years before our divorce. What type of wedding is appropriate in our case?

Both of you would probably feel more comfortable in a simple, intimate ceremony in an informal setting, with family members and a few close friends in attendance. You might consider getting married at home or in the small chapel of a church.

What about inviting ex-inlaws to my wedding? Would this be appropriate? I am thinking particularly about my former husband's parents and his sister, who has remained a very close friend.

Talk this over with your fiancé to make sure he has no objection. Then, if you feel comfortable about it and you believe your former in-laws would also feel at ease, there's no reason why you shouldn't invite them. Just make sure that their presence wouldn't bring back some bad memories of the past that would cast a cloud of gloom on this wedding. Your main concern should be to make this wedding a happy, festive occasion.

What about gifts for a second wedding?

The best approach is not to expect them and do your best to discourage them. Since you've been married before, you and your fiancé already have most of the necessities for setting up housekeeping. Some people may bring gifts anyway. If this happens, accept them graciously and acknowledge them with a personal note of thanks soon after the wedding.

Getting Ready
for the Wedding

Just like the first time around, a second wedding requires thorough preparation. Some of the important planning details are listed here for your convenience. As you complete each item, check it off and write the completion date in the appropriate space.

4-6 MONTHS BEFORE THE WEDDING

DATE
COMPLETED

_____ Talk with fiancé about type of wedding wanted; agree on budget for the wedding and how expenses will be paid . . . .   _____

_____ Consult with minister; set wedding date . . . .   _____

_____ Reserve church; review all policies concerning weddings in church building . . . .   _____

_____ Reserve meeting place for reception; select a caterer . . . .   _____

_____ Begin compiling a guest list . . . .   _____

_____ Select a florist; make arrangements for flowers . . . .   _____

_____ Select attendants, groomsmen, and ushers . . .   _____

_____ Arrange for music; consult with organist, soloist . . . .   _____

_____ Order invitations and thank-you cards . . . . . .   _____

2-3 MONTHS BEFORE THE WEDDING

____ Plan wedding ceremony,
in consultation with minister . . . . _____
____ Start writing or addressing invitations . . . . . . _____
____ Make reservations for wedding trip . . . . _____
____ Select wedding rings and have them engraved _____
____ Order wedding dress . . . . _____
____ Make arrangements for wedding photographs _____
____ Enlist people to assist at reception . . . . _____
____ Select a person to keep the guest book . . . . . . _____

1 MONTH BEFORE THE WEDDING

____ Mail invitations . . . . _____
____ Start writing thank-you notes as gifts arrive . _____
____ Buy gifts for attendants . . . . _____
____ Plan food and accommodations for out-of-
town guests . . . . _____
____ Complete all arrangements for rehearsal and
rehearsal dinner . . . . _____
____ Secure marriage license . . . . _____

2 WEEKS BEFORE THE WEDDING

____ Have the wedding bulletins printed . . . . _____
____ Double-check all details about the rehearsal
and the ceremony with the minister . . . . _____
____ Double-check all reservations and details
with florist, caterer, photographer, musi-
cians, formal wear agency, etc. . . . . _____
____ Make arrangements for someone to tape-
record ceremony; check to see that church
lighting and sound systems are working . . . . . _____

ON THE WEDDING DAY

____ Arrange to take several cars to the church to
transport clothing, gifts, guests, wedding par-
ty, etc. . . . . _____

____ Make sure church is unlocked early for wedding party; arrange for entry to dressing rooms, sanctuary, etc. . . . . _____

____ Take needle and thread, extra pins, etc., for last-minute fitting emergencies . . . . _____

____ Have fees ready to pay minister, organist, custodian, etc. . . . . _____

AFTER THE WEDDING

____ Now that it's all over, relax and enjoy your wedding trip! . . . . _____

____ Finish writing and mailing thank-you notes . . _____